Landscape Gardening

Other Publications:

*This volume is one of a series that offers information
on the cultivation of indoor and outdoor plants and explains
the principles of garden design.*

Landscape Gardening

by
James Underwood Crockett
and
the Editors of TIME-LIFE BOOKS

Watercolor Illustrations by
Rebecca A. Merrilees and Barbara Wolff

TIME-LIFE BOOKS, ALEXANDRIA, VIRGINIA

Time-Life Books Inc.
is a wholly owned subsidiary of
TIME INCORPORATED

FOUNDER: Henry R. Luce 1898-1967

Editor-in-Chief: Henry Anatole Grunwald
President: J. Richard Munro
Chairman of the Board: Ralph P. Davidson
Executive Vice President: Clifford J. Grum
Chairman, Executive Committee: James R. Shepley
Editorial Director: Ralph Graves
Group Vice President, Books: Joan D. Manley
Vice Chairman: Arthur Temple

TIME-LIFE BOOKS INC.

MANAGING EDITOR: Jerry Korn
Executive Editor: David Maness
Assistant Managing Editors: Dale M. Brown (planning),
George Constable, Martin Mann, John Paul Porter,
Gerry Schremp (acting)
Art Director: Tom Suzuki
Chief of Research: David L. Harrison
Director of Photography: Robert G. Mason
Assistant Art Director: Arnold C. Holeywell
Assistant Chief of Research: Carolyn L. Sackett
Assistant Director of Photography: Dolores A. Littles

CHAIRMAN: John D. McSweeney
President: Carl G. Jaeger
Executive Vice Presidents: John Steven Maxwell,
David J. Walsh
Vice Presidents: George Artandi (comptroller);
Stephen L. Bair (legal counsel); Peter G. Barnes;
Nicholas Benton (public relations); John L. Canova;
Beatrice T. Dobie (personnel); Carol Flaumenhaft (consumer
affairs); James L. Mercer (Europe/South Pacific);
Herbert Sorkin (production); Paul R. Stewart (marketing)

THE TIME-LIFE ENCYCLOPEDIA OF GARDENING

EDITORIAL STAFF FOR LANDSCAPE GARDENING:
EDITOR: Robert M. Jones
Assistant Editor: Carlotta Kerwin
Text Editors: Robert Tschirky, Anne Horan
Picture Editor: Jane Scholl
Designer: Leonard Wolfe
Staff Writers: Marian Gordon Goldman, Lee Greene,
Paula Pierce, Peter Wood
Chief Researcher: Joan Mebane
Researchers: Kathleen Brandes, Muriel Clarke,
Evelyn Constable, Margo Dryden, Helen Fennell,
Helen Greenway, Gail Hansberry, Mary Kay Moran,
Diana Sweeney
Design Assistant: Mervyn Clay
Staff Illustrator: Vincent Lewis
Special Contributor: Henry Moscow (text)

EDITORIAL PRODUCTION
Production Editor: Feliciano Madrid
Operations Manager: Gennaro C. Esposito,
Gordon E. Buck (assistant)
Quality Control: Robert L. Young (director),
James J. Cox (assistant), Daniel J. McSweeney,
Michael G. Wight (associates)
Art Coordinator: Anne B. Landry
Copy Staff: Susan B. Galloway (chief), Heidi Sanford,
Patricia Miller, Celia Beattie
Picture Department: Barbara S. Simon
Traffic: Kimberly K. Lewis

For information about any Time-Life book, please write:
Reader Information
Time-Life Books
541 North Fairbanks Court
Chicago, Illinois 60611

THE AUTHOR: The late James Underwood Crockett, a graduate of the University of Massachusetts, received an Honorary Doctor of Science degree from that university and was cited by the American Association of Nurserymen and the American Horticultural Society. He worked with plants in California, New York, Texas and New England. He was the author of books on greenhouse, indoor and window-sill gardening, and wrote a monthly column for *Horticulture* magazine and a monthly bulletin, "Flowery Talks," for retail florists. His weekly television program, *Crockett's Victory Garden,* was seen by more than three million viewers on 125 public broadcasting stations throughout the United States.

GENERAL CONSULTANTS: Carlton B. Lees, Vice President, New York Botanical Garden, Bronx, New York; Joseph J. Kern, Mentor, Ohio; Albert P. Nordheden, Morganville, New Jersey.

THE COVER: A landscape design for an Arizona garden leads the eye first to the pool, which reflects the clear desert sky and the spiky native shrubs, then along the sharp, strong forms of rock to the rugged beauty of the desert itself. The pool and patio were designed to take advantage of Arizona's ever-changing light, which assumes a rainbow quality when it is reflected by the varied textures, the bushy greenery and the gleaming water.

CORRESPONDENTS: Elisabeth Kraemer (Bonn); Margot
Hapgood, Dorothy Bacon, Lesley Coleman (London); Susan
Jonas, Lucy T. Voulgaris (New York); Maria Vincenza Aloisi,
Josephine du Brusle (Paris); Ann Natanson (Rome). Valuable
assistance was also provided by: Sue Wymelenberg (Boston);
William McK. Chapman (Charleston, S.C.); Holland
McCombs (Dallas); Judy Aspinall (London); Jessica Silvers
(Los Angeles); Patricia Chandler (New Orleans); Carolyn T.
Chubet, Miriam Hsia, Christina Lieberman (New York);
Jocelyn Cox (Portland, Oregon); Mimi Murphy (Rome);
Martha Green (San Francisco); Jane Estes (Seattle).

Library of Congress Cataloguing in Publication Data
Crockett, James Underwood.
    Landscape gardening, by James Underwood Crockett and
    the editors of Time-Life Books. Watercolor illus. by
    Rebecca A. Merrilees and Barbara Wolff. New York,
    Time-Life Books [1971]
    160 p. illus. (part col.), col. plan. 28 cm. (The Time-Life
    encyclopedia of gardening)
    1. Landscape gardening.   I. Time-Life Books.   II. Title.
SB473.C76   712'.6   77-26564
ISBN 0-8094-1088-5
ISBN 0-8094-1090-7 lib. bdg.
ISBN 0-8094-1089-3 ret. ed.

CONTENTS

What landscaping can do 1

Occasionally when I drive past one of those monotonous housing developments that exist everywhere, I try to imagine how different landscape architects would treat a row of houses like these, and remove the sameness from them. Take a typical street in one of the big developments: five nearly identical houses placed squarely in the middle of five identical lots. In my mind's eye I see how landscaping could make the five houses look quite different—and, more important, different in ways that make each home better suited to the needs and personality of its owner.

One landscape designer would plant more trees and shrubs all around the house, de-emphasizing it and providing more privacy for the side and back yards. The landscape architect working next door might run a driveway in a crescent in front of the house and plant trees so as to frame it and make it appear larger than it is. When you drove past you would never know these two houses were similar. At the next address another landscape architect would set an attractive garden near the front door, with a hedge-bordered flagstone walk beckoning you to the doorway. And next door another designer would carry the flagstone walk past the side of the house and into an inviting garden where a glimpse of a patio and outdoor grill hinted at party gaiety. The fifth house would be set in a veritable grove of trees, by a landscape architect whose client wanted country quiet and seclusion for his suburban house.

A homeowner who cherishes his privacy; another who wants his house to look impressive; another who wants to make it particularly inviting; another who wants the convenience of back-yard informality; and a fifth who likes to live in the woods—all five would express their personalities in the landscaping of their homes. And instead of a monotonous row of houses looking all the same, that particular street would have both an esthetic and a functional quality that made life all the more pleasant, for the passerby as well as the homeowner. That is what landscaping is all about.

This basic purpose of landscaping—the creation of a pleas-

Only 50 feet wide, a lot in Dallas, Texas, was made into a cool, spacious private garden with a wood walk and deck, ground covers and little grass, and a vine-covered wire fence that admits the breeze.

ant, functional, personal environment—is increasingly recognized by the people I have met as I traveled around the country. In the course of working on this book, I visited dozens of gardens, many of them exquisitely designed, and talked to their owners and landscape architects. They spoke with pride of specific accomplishments— how they arranged a deck to get outdoor living on an impossible hillside lot, or how the new terrace has opened up a new way of life. They also talked of privacy and beauty and low upkeep, for these too are on people's minds today. But the most interesting things homeowners said revealed how much they have learned about landscape gardening as an art, and what it can mean in improving the quality of day-to-day living. For although their private landscapes are infinitely varied, depending on region, income and taste, the underlying principles they have made use of are the same. Those principles, once understood, can be applied by any homeowner to make his own lot a happier one.

Each of these well-designed gardens was planned in some detail before a plant was bought or a brick laid. The need for such an overall concept of the landscape is often ignored, for many people think first in terms of specific shrubs and trees; they fall in love with a blue spruce or a flowering cherry or an azalea and rush out to bring it home and get it into the ground, without always considering how it might best be used. The result of this approach can be a hodgepodge of nursery plants, hard to maintain, disappointing to look at, uncomfortable to live with.

Each plant has its own special characteristics; more than 350 particularly useful and beautiful ones are noted in the illustrated encyclopedia section beginning on page 99. One of the tricks in landscape gardening is knowing these characteristics, how they can be used to best advantage, and how plants can be combined with other materials, including paving, paths, walls, fences and the materials of the house. Then these elements can be blended to create a landscape that fits the needs of the family it serves.

This approach to landscaping is dictated by a basic change in the way Americans view its purpose. In times past it was intended primarily to please other people. This emphasis on putting up a good front became exaggerated in Victorian days, when the grounds around a house served only one purpose: show. As late as 1916, one of the country's well-known landscape architects, Robert Cridland, upheld that tradition when he lamented, "It is much to be regretted that most of our lawn area is in the rear of the house. Certainly this gives a larger measure of privacy, but too often this privacy is a detriment. People grow careless of that which is not open for all to see."

Today the hidden lawns Cridland deplored are a mark of good

landscaping. Americans are beginning to look upon their grounds not so much as a means to impress their neighbors, although this purpose will probably always persist, but as usable, livable extensions of the house itself—outdoor rooms to be treated and used in much the ways indoor rooms are. And the living spaces within the house have been turned around; they no longer face forward to the street but backward to the rear garden.

This change in outlook has come about as the idea of outdoor living, developed in California, was applied across the country to the need for a secluded retreat from urban pressures. The result was the transformation of the back yard, which is no longer a place for clotheslines, garbage cans and vegetable gardens, but a natural setting for relaxation, meals, parties and family games. Service functions, such as storage of fireplace logs and tools, have been compressed into small efficient spaces or integrated into multipurpose areas. And the front yard, slowest of all to change, is gradually losing its role as a showpiece. In most instances it still supplies its share of the attractive plantings that a neighborhood displays to the public, but increasingly it is becoming a semiprivate area for welcoming visitors, who today do not arrive on foot but in cars, which have to be parked.

This new concept of the home seeks to achieve six main goals through landscaping:

Privacy. Most people want their houses and grounds to provide some sense of shelter from the crowding and tension of an urban world—a place where ties come off, and shirts too; where tired feet can be soothed by cool grass; where green foliage helps the mind forget highway traffic. They seek seclusion, yet not at the cost of a feeling of confinement.

Comfort. The house is there to shelter you from the weather; the grounds ought to allow you to enjoy it. Trees can filter bright sunlight and absorb its heat—the temperature beneath a tree may be 15° to 20° lower than in the sun. A row of trees and shrubs will absorb annoying winds, creating on its leeward side a sheltered space several times its own height. Thick foliage can also suppress street noise and even capture pollutants from the air while freshening it with oxygen.

Beauty. Whatever you see outdoors from wherever you stand in your house or on your grounds is your landscape, whether or not you own what you are looking at. Good planning can include a neighbor's beautiful tree in this landscape, while screening out his garage. Making your own garden attractive for you and for passersby depends on attention to details: the combination of plant forms, colors and textures of leaves, grass and paths to create interesting contrasts; the placement of plants to lead the eye to bright

A MANUFACTURED MOUNTAIN

Among the most wildly extravagant landscaping jobs ever devised were the fabled Hanging Gardens of Babylon, one of the seven wonders of the ancient world. They were constructed on the hot plain of the Euphrates Valley during the Sixth Century B.C. by the all-powerful ruler Nebuchadnezzar to assuage the homesickness of his mountain-born queen. According to most accounts, they resembled a huge man-made mountain with gardens planted on a series of wide setback terraces. Supporting the terraces were immense hollow arches of sun-baked brick, waterproofed inside with asphalt and sheets of lead and filled with topsoil to accommodate the deep-reaching roots of large cedar, cypress, larch, mimosa and palm trees. These, and a profusion of bushes and flowering vines that hung over the terraces, were kept green with water pumped from the Euphrates River to the top by slaves; from there, it flowed down through an artfully designed irrigation system that included fountains. Underneath the terraces were royal apartments where Nebuchadnezzar and his queen could enjoy their mountain in comfort.

points of interest and to suggest spaciousness; the selection of trees and shrubs to be good-looking in winter as well as summer.

Convenience and safety. If you have ever found yourself at someone's back door when you meant to arrive at his front door, you understand the necessity for functional design. Paths must not meander meaninglessly, and guests should not have to walk through the kitchen, or worse still, through a garage, to get to a garden; both walks and doorways should be determined by a logical traffic pattern. Steps should be lighted for safety, and the design of treads and risers should make for easy climbing. Shrubs should be planted so that they will not overhang walks to snag clothing, shower dew or rain on passersby, and, in cold climates, hinder snow removal. Service areas should provide convenient storage for accumulated trash, garden equipment and large toys, as well as spaces for clotheslines and compost piles.

Ease of maintenance. I used to give the boy on the next block a quarter to mow my lawn; now the price is five dollars, and I mow it myself. You can be sure that I have taken steps to make the job

MANIPULATING SPACE

No matter what the size or shape of a lot, landscaping can create useful outdoor areas that also provide a sense of spaciousness, visual interest and elements of surprise. On an extremely shallow lot (1) outdoor spaces can be arranged on an axis parallel to the back lot line: a paved terrace screened from neighboring lots by a fence opens onto a small promenade of grass flanked by rows of trees, which are interrupted at one point to provide a visual outlet and to give access to the lawn at the front of the lot. On a squarish lot (2) the longest dimension, the diagonal, is used to provide a feeling of greater space as well as to stimulate the observer's interest: from the well-shielded terrace the eye is led out and then around a corner, through a break in the plantings, toward the street. There is even room for a vegetable garden tucked away in the upper-right corner of the lot. On a long, narrow lot (3) a bowling-alley effect is avoided by dividing the space into two distinct areas: an intimate patio, which is enclosed by low hedges and ornamental trees, and an open area of lawn and garden.

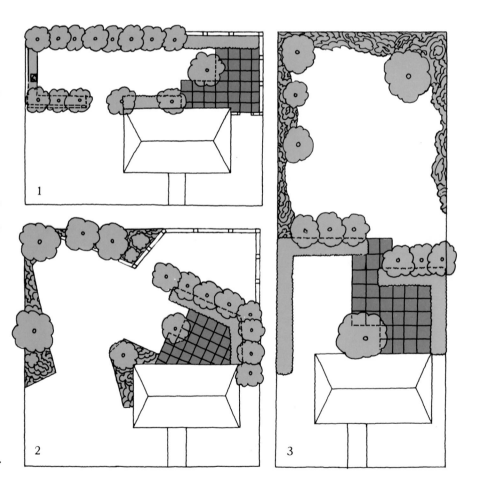

easy. There are now few beds or shrubs to get around, and the main beds have mowing strips—flat borders of brick or stone laid between them and the lawn—to eliminate tedious edging. But lawns are seldom as much trouble as plants that have been chosen without thought of the care they need. Planting a fast-growing shrub that requires continual pruning may be a mistake when a slow-growing variety would serve better. Raised planting beds and plant containers can make gardening easier, not only because they reduce the amount of stooping necessary, but because they eliminate the problem of grass invading flower beds (and make it unlikely that children will trample through the flowers looking for a lost ball). Whether beds are raised or not, the use of mulches and low ground-covering plants can help unify taller plantings visually and at the same time hold needed moisture and restrict the growth of weeds, reducing both watering and weeding chores. In especially dry climates, an automatic underground watering system may prove a worthwhile laborsaving investment.

Flexibility. The most useful gardens are those that allow for a variety of activities in the same area. The service yard can conceal garbage pails while providing space for a vegetable garden, and an open expanse of lawn can be a court for badminton in the afternoon, a site for a supper party in the evening, and all the rest of the time something pleasant to look at. But flexibility is also essential because change is inevitable in a garden. Not only do plants continue to grow but family needs change as well. When children graduate from the sandbox, the sandbox may have to be removed or converted into a flower bed. The plastic wading pool for toddlers may be replaced by a family swimming pool; in this case, it is wise to plan a spot for the pool well ahead of time, and to leave access for the heavy machines that will be needed to build it.

These six goals are the ones that most people agree on. But the only essential goal is a landscape that will please its inhabitants, and every family has its own priorities. Before buying a single shrub, then, I suggest you take these steps:

Look out the windows of your house, and note what you see. Are the main views from living room, kitchen and other major areas ones that you like to look at? If not, might they be improved by planting or construction to add something attractive or hide something unattractive? Go out into the back yard and the front yard, look back at the house and make the same assessment.

Sit down of an evening and discuss what each member of the family thinks is good and bad about the house and grounds, and what they would like to see changed. As your priorities start to become clearer in your mind, see what other people have done. You will generally get the best ideas from professionally designed gardens, where you stand a better chance of seeing how problems have been well solved. Keep an eye out for house and garden tours, organized from time to time by garden clubs, horticultural societies and charitable organizations; they afford you a chance to visit gardens you would otherwise never see. I never cease to enjoy doing this, both around Boston and when I happen to be visiting another city. The tours are tremendously popular, and I always see many wives with their husbands along, often with a camera to record ideas that appeal to them. To become more knowledgeable about plant materials and design, I also suggest that you visit nearby "demonstration gardens," which are sponsored in many regions by garden clubs, botanic gardens, municipal arboretums and some of the larger nurseries. With such homework done, you are in a much better position to assess your own house and grounds and decide what can be left as is, what should be removed and added, and what to include in a plan that can be budgeted and carried out over a period of one, two or even five years.

The plan itself ought to be drawn up, starting with a rough map of your house and grounds as they exist. To make one, you need a 50- or 100-foot measuring tape and someone to hold the other end. Measure and record the dimensions of the house, including the locations of windows and entrances, then the position of major trees, driveway, walks, walls, property lines and other fixed features. Using these measurements, sketch out a bird's-eye view of the house and grounds. Even if you lack drafting skill, you can make a useful map showing all features in their proper proportions by drawing on graph paper, which is marked off into squares and can be bought at a stationery or art supply store; a 17-by-22-inch sheet that has either 8 squares to the inch or 10 squares to the inch is convenient—if each square represents 1 square foot on the ground, one sheet with 8 squares to the inch will suffice for a map of a lot as large as 136 by 176 feet; a sheet with 10 squares to the inch for 170 by 220 feet. Also buy a pad of tracing paper of the same or slightly larger size (some pads come with the sheet of graph paper included). Slip the graph paper with the drawing of your grounds under a sheet of tracing paper, or tape both to a piece of stiff board. Then you are ready to start sketching landscape changes on the tracing paper over the map of existing features. Don't erase unsatisfactory sketches. Start again with a fresh sheet of tracing overlay and keep your discards—you may want to come back to them later. Working this way allows you to try different landscaping ideas—on paper, where mistakes cost nothing, progressing from lot map to rough analysis to final plan (right). The more you experiment in drawings beforehand, the less chance there is for

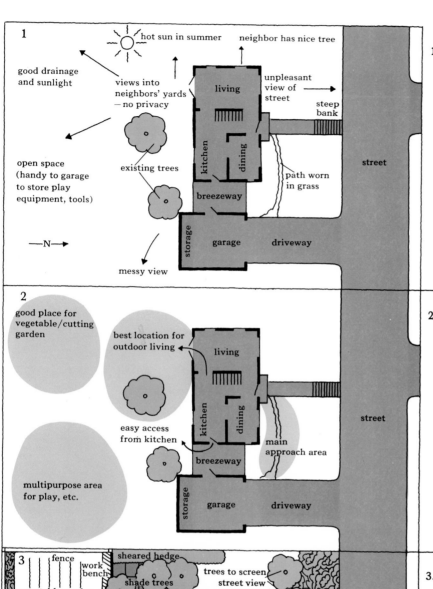

1 — *Panel 1 labels:*
hot sun in summer
neighbor has nice tree
good drainage and sunlight
views into neighbors' yards — no privacy
unpleasant view of street
living
steep bank
kitchen
dining
street
existing trees
path worn in grass
open space (handy to garage to store play equipment, tools)
breezeway
storage
garage
driveway
→ N →
messy view

2 — *Panel 2 labels:*
good place for vegetable/cutting garden
best location for outdoor living
living
kitchen
dining
street
easy access from kitchen
main approach area
breezeway
multipurpose area for play, etc.
storage
garage
driveway

3 — *Panel 3 labels:*
fence
work bench
sheared hedge
shade trees
trees to screen street view
vegetable garden
tools
living
ground cover
paved patio
wire fence with flowering vine
kitchen
dining
street
flower border against fence
flowers
lawn
breezeway
flowering tree
flowering tree
storage
garage
driveway
informal hedge
lawn

GETTING A PLAN ON PAPER

1. *A homeowner who is considering landscaping changes can avoid mistakes and improve results by first making an analysis on paper. Start by measuring house and grounds; then draw a map of existing conditions like the one shown in the sketch at the left. Include the location of doors and windows, driveways and paths, trees and other major plantings, the effect of sun, good views and bad ones, and problems that need attention. Draw the plan on a graph-paper grid, letting each square represent 1 square foot, or, on large lots, 4 square feet.*

2. *As a second step, place tracing paper over the map and rough in possible uses for different areas. In this example, the area in back of the garage is the logical place to keep as open lawn, conveniently near game equipment and toys stored in the garage. A sunny, well-drained back corner of the lot is earmarked for a vegetable garden. Space right outside the living room and conveniently near the kitchen will become the outdoor living-dining area. And a new approach is needed where a path has been worn in the grass between driveway and front door.*

3. *When functional areas have been determined, experiment with actual designs on fresh sheets of tracing paper laid over the map. At left is one way a solution might look. The new terrace is shielded from the neighbors' view by a hedge, from the sun by trees, and from the vegetable garden by a storage cabinet and workbench. Terrace paving extends as a path to the kitchen. In front, a new entrance terrace serves the front door and the breezeway and kitchen. New trees screen bad views, and a steep, hard-to-mow bank is planted in a ground cover.*

oversight later on. If someday you hear yourself saying, "How many times have I told you kids to stay out of the petunias!" you put either the petunia bed or the play area in the wrong place.

ORGANIZING YOUR GROUNDS   The heart of any good landscaping plan is its organization of space to provide a number of areas, each serving a well-defined purpose and adding to the overall usefulness as well as beauty of the grounds. The location of the house on the lot is the first factor defining separate areas on the lot. Generally you cannot change that, and it will affect the way you organize the remaining grounds. Most people divide the grounds into three main areas: a semipublic entrance area, a private living area and a service area.

This scheme corresponds quite closely to the way in which most houses are arranged inside. There is usually a small hall or foyer at the entrance; the largest part is the living area, including rooms for dining, recreation and entertaining; service areas provide for kitchen, laundry and perhaps a shop in the basement.

The corresponding indoor and outdoor areas should be close to one another, allowing easy access from an area inside to its counterpart outdoors. Integrating spaces, indoors and out, requires careful planning of patios and terraces, walks and driveways, as well as the most sensible use of existing doors (and if necessary, new ones). But organizing and locating your outdoor areas carefully, as described in detail in the following chapters, can enhance your pleasure and use of both house and grounds.

Within each of the areas making up a plan, the six basic goals of landscaping apply. The materials available to achieve them include a great number of different plant materials—trees, shrubs, vines and ground-cover plants—as well as countless materials for fences, walls, terraces and walks. Using them to best advantage can be simplified if you keep in mind a few principles.

Plan in the abstract. Landscape designers view plants and other materials as generalized forms, concentrating on the broad characteristics of shape, texture and color rather than on details of individual types. To achieve privacy, for example, you need something that is fairly tall and that does not take too much space from the rest of the yard. A wooden fence will serve, as will a hedge of privet—but so too will a row of lilac bushes, a string of low-branching dogwood or flowering crab-apple trees, or an appropriately placed storage shed. Texture, too, influences use; fine-leaved willow trees cast a pattern of light shade, while the broad, overlapping leaves of a maple create a cool, dark retreat from the sun. Both shape and texture affect appearance, as does color, which varies more among green plants than many people realize. Careful harmonizing of shapes, textures and colors can do more to create an attractive outdoor setting than costly investments in unusual plants.

Keep the design in scale. As a general rule, but one with many exceptions, small houses look best with small plants and modest garden structures. One of the most common errors in home landscaping is to select shrubs and trees that will grow too large. A 6-foot spruce may look quite attractive beside the front steps—at first. But don't put one there, as many homeowners have done, because it may eventually reach 70 feet in height, with a spread of 40 feet.

Keep things simple. If you choose plant materials and combine them carefully, they will provide an ever-changing panorama through the year. Each major area should have some sort of focal point, some especially handsome element to which attention is drawn, whether it is a fine front door or a piece of sculpture or a bed of brilliant flowers or a single, shimmering tree. But avoid at all costs having too many focal points, as they will tend to cancel one another out and cause visual confusion. Too great a variety among plantings is distracting, while repetition of similar shapes, textures and colors tends to be pleasing. A rule that was old when I started as a nurseryman still holds. Never buy more than three or four types of plants for any one planting, and never buy one of anything unless it is worth the spotlight of attention all by itself.

These principles are very general ones. They can be applied to any style house in any part of the country. And they work in all areas of a landscape plan. In fact, their use in a side yard in southern Ohio impressed their effectiveness on me.

The house was a style popular in the '20s, with the kitchen on the side. The window over the sink faced west, looking out on the next-door neighbor's driveway, and the owner's wife complained that not only did she stare at a dreary view but the afternoon sun was unpleasant. A row of shrubs had been planted next to the house, but they were no help—all they did was block the lower edge of the windows. The owner asked a landscape designer friend for advice. His solution was simple, very practical—and charming.

He removed the shrubs and replaced them with a brick walk, bordered on the far side by a bed of orange and yellow marigolds, which look bright and provide fresh cut flowers for the house. The short stretch from the walk to the boundary line was lawn, and that was left unchanged. But along the boundary he planted six flowering crab apples. They shade the house wall in summer and even in winter their graceful bare branches break up the view of the driveway. Now the housewife working at her sink looks out on a private garden: colorful blossoms in spring, green leaves and flowers all summer long, a lovely pattern of branches in winter—and all year round a vivid show from birds attracted by the trees' fruit and a bird feeder hung from one of them.

WHO THE PROS ARE

Helpful advice on landscaping can be obtained from nurserymen and landscape contractors, who sell and install plants and carry out details of garden construction. For professional assistance in garden design, there are in addition some 4,000 landscape architects in the U.S. and Canada; they are licensed by some states and provinces and most hold a master's or bachelor's degree in landscape architecture from a professionally accredited college or university. Landscape architects provide a full range of services, from site analysis to working drawings to supervision of plantings; fees are based on an hourly scale, a lump sum or a percentage of costs. Although many landscape architects find it difficult to break even on smaller residential design jobs, some welcome them and others will consult on an hourly basis without committing a client to the full range of services.

A legacy from Europe's gardens

On a chilly March day in 1621 the newly arrived Pilgrims planted the precious garden seeds they had brought with them on the *Mayflower;* in so doing, they established one of the three basic patterns that influenced the colonial gardens of America—patterns that in modern forms can be glimpsed in some of the gardens in this book. From the Pilgrims' seeds sprang the modest dooryard gardens of Plymouth, which were modeled after the cottage gardens of England and which spread westward to become the prototypes for the American front yard. The first dooryard gardens were fenced-in spaces conveniently located near the kitchen door. Every plant filled a practical need: there were not only vegetables and spices but plants like "bouncing Bet" for shrinking wool, St.-John's-wort for treating sciatica and witches' spells, and tansy, valued as a food flavoring and a cure for worms. As New Englanders gained affluence, however, their dooryard gardens became more decorative and were increasingly used for outdoor relaxation—so much so, in fact, that Connecticut passed a law banning Sunday garden strolling as a sinful pleasure.

There were no such taboos elsewhere in the New World. Long before the Pilgrims' arrival, the conquistadors and their missionaries had begun adapting Spanish gardens, so well suited for a hot, dry climate, to the similar conditions of Mexico and the Southwest. What emerged was the Spanish colonial garden, an enclosed patio that was as intimate a part of the house as any of its rooms. Here a bubbling fountain and vine-covered arcades offered a cool oasis from summer heat by day and a romantic setting for candlelit strolling by night.

Strolling and ostentation were the main reasons for the elegant gardens of Williamsburg, Virginia. Reflecting the influence of formal 16th and 17th Century Dutch and Flemish gardens *(opposite),* they were arranged in geometrically shaped segments called parterres, separated by walks and decorated with elaborately trimmed trees and shrubs. This formal grandeur made Williamsburg's landscapes, now faithfully reconstructed, among the most impressive in colonial America.

Workers in a 16th Century Flemish garden prepare parterres and a bower in an engraved detail of a Bruegel scene.

The show place of colonial America was Williamsburg, the capital and social center of old Virginia. The wealthy owners of its gracious town houses vied with one another in laying out artfully patterned gardens, like the one shown below, modeled after the formal Dutch gardens that were the vogue in England during the reign of Dutch-born King William III and his English Queen Mary. The grandest gardens of Williamsburg were the 12 formal pleasure areas surrounding the handsome Governor's Palace *(opposite, below)*, lavishly landscaped in the style of the English mansions of the William and Mary period *(opposite, above)*. The gardens took 12 years to finish and complaints about the cost were so widespread that Governor Alexander Spotswood volunteered in the year 1718 "if the Assembly did not care to be at Expence of the Fish-Pond & Falling Gardens, to take them to my Self." The palace and its gardens were destroyed by fire in 1781, but have been fully reconstructed and serve today, with restored Williamsburg, as a living monument to an elegant era.

The flower-filled triangular beds of Williamsburg's Custis-Maupin Garden (left), each bordered with boxwood hedges and separated by brick walks, resemble a modified British flag when seen from above.

An old engraving of Mount Morris, an English mansion built around 1680, when the Dutch influence on English gardening was at its height, shows Dutch technique in the elaborate parterres and sculptured shrubbery of its front and rear pleasure gardens, which are walled for privacy.

The diamond-shaped hedges and cylindrical shrubs of the elegant Ballroom Garden are seen in this view from the Governor's Palace in Williamsburg. Beyond, a few steps lower, is the North Garden, with its tree-lined allée, or aisle, flanked by a pair of magnificent tulip beds.

The New England dooryard garden

All the plants in the Whipple House garden—herbs, strawberries and even roses—were put to practical uses.

An illustration for a popular English gardening book of the early 17th Century shows workers demonstrating the proper techniques for transplanting trees and shrubs into raised beds (below) and for pleaching, or weaving, vines onto an arbor (above) that provided a shady area.

This maple-framed view of the front of the Whipple House shows a number of the dooryard garden plantings spilling beyond the limits of the rustic split paling fence. Fences of this kind, usually higher, were used around colonial dooryard gardens to keep out foraging livestock.

By 1640, when the Whipple House was built in Ipswich, Massachusetts, New England dooryard gardens had begun to lose some of the purely functional character that marked their Pilgrim prototypes. The reconstructed Whipple House garden pictured here, with its raised beds and walks, reflects the influence of English gardening manuals of the period (top).

More than 5,000 miles, six centuries and a king's fortune separate the modern Texas patio garden shown at right, below, from its splendid Moorish ancestor in Spain's Alhambra Palace *(opposite, top)*. Yet they share the basic elements that made enclosed gardens refuges of beauty and comfort in hot, dry climates as far back as the days of ancient Egypt and Persia: water, green plants and shady arcades. The conquering Moors introduced their beautiful Persian-inspired gardens to Spain in the 10th Century. They built so many of them in Granada that a charmed visitor described the city as "a goblet full of emeralds." After the expulsion of the Moors from Spain in the 1400s, the Spanish added their own touches—more elaborate fountains, grottoes, statuary—to the basic Moorish design. They also substituted clusters of colorful, fragrant native plants for the Moors' closely trimmed shrubs and fruit trees. The result was a typically Spanish patio garden, little different from the one shown below, which was enjoyed by officials of the Spanish province of Texas more than 250 years ago.

The Spanish patio

A view of the patio in the restored Spanish Governor's Palace in San Antonio, Texas (left), shows the pebbled mosaic surface between the pool, with its potted acalyphas, and the vine-covered arcade.

The Alhambra's Court of the Myrtles, seen in this early 18th Century print, was named for the myrtle hedges flanking the reflecting pool. It is one of several such courts built within the walls of the fortified palace that was once the seat of Spain's Moorish kings.

The inviting Spanish-Mexican garden of a private home in San Antonio is centered on a geranium-decorated fountain and a live oak that grows in a bed of flowers and plants behind the fountain. Broad-leaved banana plants decorate the borders.

The outdoor family room 2

If you are like the people I know, you will sooner or later put most of your landscaping money and effort into that area of your property where you can comfortably live outdoors. And on most properties this means the back yard, the largest and therefore the most flexible outdoor space. It is also usually the most private. Unlike the front of the house, which you must share with the public at least to some degree, it is the one place that you can design and live in to please yourself.

To some people a space for outdoor living means a quiet oasis, a small green world where they can refresh themselves; to others it is a free-swinging activities area, a place to swim or practice chip shots. One golf fanatic I know has a regulation sand trap just off his patio, and I once visited a railroad buff whose back yard was overwhelmed by an operating signal tower.

But most outdoor spaces are intended for much the same kinds of activities as indoor ones—relaxation, eating, entertaining, games —and it is helpful to think of them in those terms. Such an outdoor living space is like an indoor "family room," one of those flexible and durable places designed to accommodate everything from family meals and informal dinner parties to messy projects and impromptu games. An outdoor family room can perform many of the same functions, as well as some strictly outdoor ones, if it is designed as a similarly flexible, all-purpose kind of space, adaptable to changing needs, easy to maintain, and, where necessary, sheltered from sun, wind and the neighbors' eyes.

To function this way, an outdoor room must have the same basic elements that its indoor counterpart has: floor, ceiling and walls. They will not be as all-enclosing as the floor, ceiling and walls of an indoor room, but they will perform very much the same tasks. And because they form the basic structure of the outdoor room, those parts of the elements that already exist must be taken into account during the planning stage. The house itself, for example, provides some of the walls for the outdoor living room, and gen-

Two chairs and a table, set informally on a small wooden deck in the shade of an old live oak, give the owners of a home in Hillsborough, California, a quiet place to sit and a fresh view of poolside activities.

erally little can be done about changing them. Existing trees must usually be counted on for part of the ceiling; which ones—if any—ought to be cut down will have major influence in determining layout. But other elements need not be considered until later. The furnishings of the outdoor space—the purely decorative plants, flowers, pools, lighting, statuary or whatever, as well as the actual outdoor furniture—are, like the furnishings of a house, concerns to be taken up after the basic plan of the room has been worked out to the satisfaction of the prospective users.

THE OUTDOOR ROOM
A well-designed outdoor room can be a single area behind the house, but more likely it will be divided into two areas: one for intensive use—generally a paved terrace near the house for sitting, dining and some children's play—and a larger adjoining area that gets lighter wear but can be used for almost anything—an occasional game of catch or badminton with the kids, an overflow of guests from the terrace during a party, or just looking at to enjoy the feeling of spaciousness it gives.

The layout of these areas depends partly on the design of the house interior. The outdoor room must be easy to reach from indoors—ideally, it will be a physical extension of indoor living spaces. If you have to go out a front or side door and then around the house to get to it, or if you have to go through several rooms or lead your guests through the kitchen to find it, the outdoor room probably will not be used very much, even if you spend a fortune on it. So if your yard is not an easy step or two from living room, dining room or back hall, it will almost certainly be worth the expense, generally a modest one, to convert a rear window into a door.

The location of the access to the back yard usually determines the location of the terrace section. If this space is kept close to the kitchen, meals and drinks can be served with a minimum of walking back and forth. Of course there are exceptions to the rule requiring the terrace to be close to the refrigerator; if by walking to another part of your property you can gain a much better view, say of a lovely river valley, it would be silly to ignore that location and build the terrace next to the house simply to have it handy to the kitchen. Or, if you happen to be blessed with a magnificent old shade tree that is not right near the house, a path to a terrace there might be well worth the extra steps.

It is easier to be explicit about the size and shape of a terrace. For convenient use by a few people—say a party of six or eight—it should be at least 12 feet on a side, preferably 15 feet, and more square or round than oblong to allow for natural furniture groupings and room to move around in. A terrace that is 20 or even 30 feet across is still better; it will permit the entertaining of a large group on a summer evening, and it will also be roomy enough to do double duty as a children's play area, one that is easily supervised from windows of the house.

For the larger open space beyond the terrace the main criteria are just that—large if possible and in any case open. A yard dotted with trees and shrubs placed at random becomes an obstacle course that is difficult if not impossible to play touch football or croquet on and, if planted in grass, an eternal nuisance to mow.

Thoughtful advance planning of the layout makes possible wide latitude in the choice of materials for the walls, ceiling and floor of the outdoor living space. Flooring, for example, can be of wood, cut stone, gravel, tile, even a layer of wood chips for particular areas. But grass is still the best all-round surfacing for the main open space, except, perhaps, in the smallest city gardens and in the most arid areas of the West and Southwest. Grass is pleasant to look at, resilient and comfortable underfoot—children can tumble on it repeatedly without hurting themselves—and it is the easiest and least expensive material to install. Its restful green color not only looks cool; on a hot day grass *is* cool, acting as a natural air conditioner by giving off moisture that lowers the temperature appreciably near its surface. An area of open lawn can also act as a unifying visual element, providing a smooth, neutral setting for the stronger shapes, colors and textures of paving, fences, trees, shrubs and flowers.

Grass, of course, requires a certain amount of mowing, fertilizing and watering, but such maintenance need not become a lifework. The most important thing is to choose the right grass in the first place. Not all lawn grasses flourish in all climates. A combination of bluegrasses and fescues, for example, is usually best in the cool regions of the northern states and southern Canada, but would soon wither in the heat of the Deep South and the Southwest, where Bermuda grass or Zoysia would be a better choice.

Local conditions are the principal consideration in grass selection. Beyond that, simply buy the best grade you can afford. It is seldom necessary to use different types for different areas within a garden, choosing one for a shady spot, another for sunny sections and still another for spaces that get heavy use.

Most cool-area lawns are grown from seeds (rather than sod, plugs or sprigs), and most of the seeds sold are mixtures of sun-loving and shade-tolerant grasses. When you sow a mixture, a process of natural selection will take place. From among its several types the one best suited to the sun, soil and moisture of a particular section of your lawn takes over and becomes dominant there. Other types take over elsewhere, giving a lawn whose characteristics vary from section to section and suit the conditions in every spot. The

FLOORS FOR OUTDOORS

BROOKLYN'S FAMOUS TREE

Its Latin name, Ailanthus altissima, means "tree of heaven," but it is best known as the "tree that grew in Brooklyn," after the 1943 novel by Betty Smith—a fast-growing species that defies grime, urban pollution, insects and even prejudice. Today it is disdained as a weed, but once it was a prized specimen, highly acclaimed as an exotic and useful addition to the urban landscape. A native of northern China, the ailanthus arrived on these shores via England in the late 18th Century, and soon many a street and front yard basked in the shade of its graceful, fernlike leaves. But its very success condemned it. It grew rapidly, up to 8 feet a year as a sapling, and its light, wind-borne seeds spread like wildfire. Sprouting in trashy back yards, on rubbish heaps, even in the cracks in sidewalks, it gained a reputation as a slum tree. Yet its stubborn tenacity has earned it a grudging affection in the green-starved hearts of city dwellers.

better grades of seed produce lawns entirely of fine-bladed grasses, which are not only the handsomest to look at but, in modern varieties, have proved rugged enough for almost any use.

GROUND COVERS   While grass is justifiably the general choice for flooring in an outdoor room, there are often reasons—esthetic as well as practical—for using other types of ground-covering plants—ivy, periwinkle, pachysandra, euonymus, for example. Such ground covers provide bold textures to contrast with the velvety smoothness of grass. They can be used in borders beside a lawn, path or terrace, or in plant beds as a patterned background for taller plants or flowers; in a bed they not only will help unify the other plants visually but will shade the ground and thereby retain moisture for the roots. Ground covers such as thyme and sandwort can be planted around a paved terrace and between stones to soften the outlines of the paving. Others, however, must be located out of the way of traffic because few of them can stand trampling.

In addition to decorative appearance, ground covers also solve particular landscaping problems. Shade-tolerant ones such as ivy and pachysandra are often the only plants that will grow in the dense shade of a tree; planted in a bed around the base of the tree, moreover, they emphasize it as a focal point in the garden. Most ground covers are well suited to planting on steep slopes, where grass would be difficult to mow; they also control erosion better than grass because their leaves break the force of rain and their roots dig deeper to hold the soil. Plants such as bearberry and juniper will grow in thin soil over rock ledges or between stones set in a rock garden, and are often used in these situations for both erosion control and the decorative contrast they provide with rock surfaces. Many ground covers, including periwinkle, sand strawberry and moss phlox, provide the bonus of flowers, and thus are especially desirable in borders near paths, steps and terraces. And finally, most ground covers can virtually be planted and forgotten about; except for an occasional watering and trimming of errant shoots, they require little maintenance. (For descriptions of selected ground covers and their suitability to different uses and different regions, consult the encyclopedia section, Chapter 5.)

HEAVY-DUTY SURFACES   For terraces, paths and other heavily used areas of the outdoor room, plants are usually too delicate to serve as flooring, and hard surface materials—flagstones, concrete, masonry blocks, tiles or wood—are more practical. My two favorites are bricks and crushed stone or gravel because they fit almost any house and garden, are relatively inexpensive and can be installed by a homeowner with even modest do-it-yourself skills. The cheapest is crushed stone or gravel, which presents a natural, textured appearance, is slightly resilient underfoot and drains well. It can be used as a permanent surfacing if thin spots are renewed from time to time, or as a temporary one if you think you might want to install a paved surface on top of it later (in which case the gravel acts as the foundation and drainage bed). A 2-to-3-inch layer of gravel is generally adequate, watered and rolled with a heavy roller. To insure stability in areas where there is frost, and to get thorough drainage in hard-packed soils, 5 to 6 inches is preferable.

For a dressier and more permanent surface, it is hard to beat common building bricks. Bricks are readily available, less expensive than most other hard paving materials and have a natural-looking earthy red color (they also come in shades of brown, gray and black). In northern climates hard-fired bricks, often called face or paving bricks, are better than porous, absorbent common bricks (though more expensive) because they resist the crumbling that results from repeated freezing and thawing. All kinds of bricks are light enough (about 4 pounds apiece) for even a child to handle easily and they can be laid in many decorative patterns.

Bricks do not have to be embedded in mortar or a solid concrete base, but can simply be laid in a 2-inch bed of sand (to keep the bricks from heaving if soil moisture freezes, it is wise to provide 3 to 5 inches of coarse crushed rock underneath the sand, particularly if the soil is not sandy enough to drain quickly). After the bricks are set in the desired pattern, more sand is brushed on top until the cracks are filled. This method of setting bricks not only is simple, but allows you to build a terrace right up to or around a shade tree; water and air will still reach the tree's roots through the cracks, and if root feeding becomes necessary, you can always pull up individual bricks to insert a crowbar or root-feeder tube at the prescribed intervals. This flexibility is also a great long-range advantage: the bricks can be pulled up from their sand bed if you want to change the shape or location of your terrace or walks.

Once you have determined the best location and flooring materials for the major spaces of your back yard, you should consider where, if anywhere, you need to enclose these spaces—where to place the walls of your outdoor room. If you have a potentially nice view of a patch of woods or a valley or a far-off church spire, you may very well want to thin or add plantings to frame and accentuate it. If there is an especially handsome old tree and a stretch of lawn on your neighbor's property, there is absolutely nothing wrong with borrowing them for your own landscape to make your lot seem more spacious. Conversely, if there is an eyesore in your line of sight, you will undoubtedly want to "plant it out"—with a single evergreen

PATTERNS IN BRICK

Among the simplest and yet the handsomest paving materials used for patios, paths and service yards is common brick, laid in a 2-inch layer of sand (spread over 3 to 5 inches of coarse crushed rock if there is a drainage problem). Sketched below are some of the most popular patterns, ranging from simple designs to more complex ones; the last one requires cutting some bricks in triangular shapes.

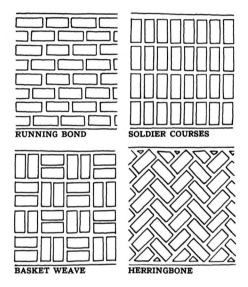

RUNNING BOND SOLDIER COURSES

BASKET WEAVE HERRINGBONE

ENCLOSING THE ROOM

or clump of evergreen shrubs like yews if the eyesore is relatively low-lying, like a neighbor's trash pile, or with taller screen planting like fast-growing pines, spruces or hemlocks if it is a higher object such as a clothesline or a television antenna.

But controlling the view is only one of the functions an outdoor wall can perform. It can simply define an area or property line, create a slight sense of enclosure or give complete privacy, make a solid backdrop for flowers and low plants, or protect against persistent winds. On many city lots, and in some parts of the country, such as California, almost totally walled- or fenced-in gardens are common, providing needed privacy in close quarters and a welcome refuge from heat, dust or wind. In most suburban situations, however, an enclosed garden is both unnecessary and undesirable (and it may be forbidden by local ordinances).

HEDGES AND SCREENS   Almost any of the functions of an outdoor wall can be served by a hedge—simply because there are so many different kinds. Although to many people the term "hedge" brings to mind a neat, formal, wall-like mass of green that must be trimmed constantly to keep it attractive, there is actually a variety of suitable plants, each with useful characteristics of its own. Some can be tightly sheared to give a formal appearance; others have a soft, feathery, informal look. Some grow into a dense barrier that will keep out almost everything but a rabbit; others remain open enough to allow wanted light and breeze to filter through. Many are highly decorative, bearing bright flowers or ornamental fruit or changing color in the fall.

For year-round privacy and wind-screening, an evergreen hedge is the best choice. A hedge of closely planted hemlocks, for example, is almost impossible to see through, winter or summer. Hemlocks have a soft look but can be sheared, if that is necessary to control the height or width. What is more, shearing hemlocks just makes their foliage thicker, a tendency not shared by spruces, which develop stubby ends like unsharpened pencils if sheared over the years. Not all evergreens, it should be noted, stay green the year around. A yew or podocarpus will keep the same color winter and summer, but American arborvitae turns a brownish green, and most red cedars turn bronze. (You may like this color change—many people do.)

Given the option of an evergreen hedge, why would anyone choose to plant a deciduous hedge? There are a number of reasons. Deciduous hedges are generally less expensive, grow faster, and many are hardier (if you want a broad-leaved hedge, a deciduous one is about your only option where winters are severe). Many provide such attractive bonuses in the landscape picture as ornamental fruit, colored autumn foliage and flowers.

There are a great many deciduous plants that make good hedges as well as taller screens. If you are interested in ornamental fall berries, brilliant red ones are borne by the American cranberry bush, the Japanese barberry and the cotoneaster. For flowers, my favorites are forsythia, rose of Sharon, hydrangea, flowering quince and spirea, which grow in lovely natural shapes but cannot be sheared into formal hedges. Both flowering quince and Japanese barberry have threatening thorns that also make them good as physical barriers. Among plants that have such thick, twiggy growth that they provide a fair visual barrier even without leaves are Amur privet, winged euonymus and lilacs. The first two of these will take rather heavy pruning if they are planted near a sidewalk or boundary and have to be kept under control. If you want height in a hurry —say, to block out your neighbor's upstairs windows or to hide an unsightly telephone pole—good choices are lilacs, bush honeysuckle and mock orange (which also provide fragrant flowers), or California privet. If you are looking for a hedge that will tolerate polluted air, in the city or on a heavily traveled street in a suburban development, try Japanese barberry—it has green or purple foliage, depending on the variety, that turns a handsome red in fall.

In relatively mild climates, there are still other choices among the broad-leaved evergreens, which provide striking foliage tex-

HOW WINDBREAKS AFFECT TEMPERATURES

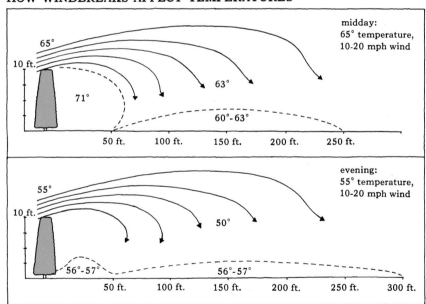

Windbreaks warm—as well as cool —outdoor living areas, as is shown in this diagram of the influence of a 10-foot hedge. At midday, the air in its lee may be 6° warmer than air to windward. Beyond, air chilled by eddying over the hedge sinks to provide cool spots on warm days. In the evening, the windbreak cools the upper air, but allows low-lying air, where plants grow, to be warmed by heat radiated from the ground.

tures. In this group, plants that will accept shearing—although they cannot be pruned as much as needled evergreens—are cherry laurel and Japanese privet. Boxwood can be sheared, but many people prefer it in its billowing natural shape. For an unpruned hedge, glossy abelia and Burford holly provide graceful, arching branches and dense coverage all the way down to the ground, and wintergreen barberry provides an excellent thorny barrier.

FENCES AND WALLS   If you need still greater privacy or wind protection than a hedge can provide, particularly if you need it immediately, the most practical answer is to build a section of fence or wall. A fence or wall, being only a few inches wide, takes up less valuable ground space than a hedge or a row of shrubs or trees, and it is for this reason sometimes the only solution where space is limited. But do not start work before checking into local zoning laws, which may stipulate what is permitted and what is not. It is also a wise precaution to talk to your neighbor or neighbors on the sides in question. They too will be affected by any barrier, and agreement in the beginning can avoid bad feelings later; it may even lead to a joint planting or fencing project and a sharing of expenses.

Masonry walls are relatively permanent and can be extremely attractive-looking, particularly if the bricks or blocks are set in an open, decorative checkerboard pattern so that light, breeze and some sense of space can come through *(page 84)*. When it comes to fences, the patterns and materials are almost unlimited. The main trick is to choose the appropriate fence for the job. A low post-and-rail fence, for example, is adequate for defining a boundary line or for supporting vines or climbing roses, but it is virtually useless for privacy screening. Conversely, a high, solid fence of palings or boards, which is good for achieving total privacy or wind control for a service yard or terrace, can create an unwelcome stockade effect if it is used to surround the entire yard.

VINES FOR SCREENING   If the main value expected from an outdoor wall is screening—or if an existing wall must itself be hidden—do not overlook vines. They can be trained on minimal supports like wires or on chain-link fences to act as screens themselves or they can be used to soften the severe lines or blank faces of heavier fences or walls. The green tracery of such clinging vines as Boston ivy, English ivy, Virginia creeper and creeping fig is particularly attractive against walls. These same plants will grow against wooden fences, although their holdfasts cling so tenaciously they may tear out bits of wood if you should ever want to remove them.

Vines that are more suitable for wooden fences are the woody-stemmed ones like grapevines and porcelain ampelopsis, which attach themselves by means of curling tendrils, or twining climbers like bittersweet, which twist their main stems around supports. These vines will support themselves on openwork fences such as wire mesh, but need vertically strung wires or trellises to twine around if they are used against a smoother-surfaced fence or wall. Other vines not only provide excellent screening or pattern effects but also produce decorative blossoms that make them good choices near a terrace or wherever color is desired; among these are five-leaf akebia, bougainvillea, clematis, climbing honeysuckle, wisteria, silver fleecevine, morning glory and trumpet vine. Among the faster-growing vines are climbers such as Japanese hop vine, mock cucumber and several kinds of gourds; they are especially useful for creating quick temporary screening because they give good coverage within 6 to 8 weeks after their seeds are planted. However, they do not provide this coverage until midsummer and since they are annuals it is necessary to replace them every year.

The third major element of the outdoor room, and in many respects its most important one, is its ceiling—the upper boundary of the back yard's space. The ultimate ceiling, of course, is the sky, with its matchless panorama of colors and cloud patterns, sun, moon and stars. In a well-designed garden this changing backdrop is enhanced if it is properly framed and filtered by the tracery of trees, whose leaves and branches provide their own graceful patterns as well as a sense of depth and shelter. Trees are the crowning touch of a garden, not only beautiful to look at but highly useful in moderating climate and surroundings—if they are chosen and located to allow in sun and breeze and views where and when they are wanted and to exclude them where and when they are not.

THE GARDEN CEILING

Many homes, especially new ones, are set on raw, open land. If you have lived in such a house, and felt the sun boring in from the west on a hot summer afternoon, you have probably realized what an irreplaceable asset a good shade tree is. A big-leafed maple or sycamore or sweet gum will keep a house or terrace beneath it cool, and the air noticeably fresher, for a tree is a living organism constantly giving forth moisture and oxygen. A handsome tree, too, can transform the appearance of an undistinguished house. And unlike the house it will grow in size and beauty from year to year; as any real estate man will tell you, a well-established shade tree is like money in the bank.

If you are among those fortunate homeowners blessed with good trees in the right place, your worries are probably over, except for occasional thinning, feeding and cleanup. If you are not, a substantial shade tree or two from a nursery is probably the most important landscaping investment you can make. Certainly it is the first landscaping investment you should consider. Trees are the dominant visual elements in any landscape, the "bones" around which the rest of the garden is fleshed out, and should be chosen and planted at the earliest opportunity. When I built my home, I planted trees the first spring before the house was half finished so that I would gain a season's growth. Landscape architects advise their clients to do the same thing. Paving is important, all right, but when a person is doing his landscaping as he goes, he should spend his money first on things that grow. A patio or terrace can go in whenever the budget will allow, but in the meantime the trees will be growing night and day. In most parts of the country a good shade tree can be bought and transplanted successfully when it is around 16 feet tall. Although it may cost 10 times as much as one of the small "whips" most people buy, it will be high enough to sit under right away or to cast shade on west-facing windows, and the price may include delivery, planting and a guarantee.

When selecting a shade tree, consider what kind of shade you want—dense, medium, or light. In areas where summer heat is extreme for long periods, heavy shade is most desirable. It can be achieved either with a tree that has large, heavily overlapping leaves, such as a Norway maple or a Southern magnolia, or with a tree that has an abundance of small leaves, such as a live oak. Other

SUMMER SHADE AND WINTER SUN

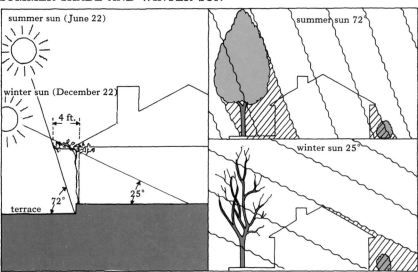

An overhead trellis, attached under the eaves of a house and covered with a deciduous vine, shields south windows from hot summer sun; in winter the leaves fall, allowing the lower rays to penetrate inside.

Similarly, a well-placed deciduous tree will shade both house and terrace in summer (top) yet allow winter sun in (bottom). Angles shown are the maximum and minimum for noon sun at 40° north latitude.

trees that give dense shade are the fruitless mulberry, linden and camphor (for descriptions of these and other trees, and illustrations of many, see Chapter 5). Bear in mind, however, that, unless thinned, such trees as they mature may cast so dense a shade that no grass will grow beneath them.

In northern areas where heat waves are of brief duration, you might better choose a tree that provides light, filtered shade by means of an open, airy structure and/or finely divided foliage. Among the best trees in this category are the honey locust, the European birch and the golden weeping willow. Under these trees, there will be sufficient light to grow grass or shade-tolerant flowers. Halfway between, with shade neither heavy nor light, is one of the most popular shade trees all across the country—the sweet gum. Other trees that give medium shade are the sycamore and Marshall's seedless ash.

In selecting a tree for shade, leaf structure is not the only consideration to keep in mind. The branches of most trees reach upward while young, but reach outward as they grow older; the more spreading the branches are at maturity, the larger the area of shade will be. The London plane tree, for example, is notable for its wide-spreading branches. Columnar trees like Lombardy poplars, on the other hand, will always remain upright and thin and are of little use for shading areas beneath them.

You should be able to walk comfortably under a mature shade tree. This means the lowest branches should be at least 7 feet above the ground. With careful pruning when the tree is young, the places where lower branches were removed will be practically invisible; removing lower branches at maturity will leave large, ugly scars. This is another reason to buy fairly large trees that have had professional nursery pruning when they were young.

The fastest-growing trees—willows, mountain ashes, silver maples—will give shade more quickly than slower-growing species, but they have relatively soft, weak wood and thus are prone to damage from wind, ice and snow. Other good shade trees like mulberries should not be used directly over a terrace; the fruit drops when it ripens and makes messy stains on the paving and furniture below. Olive trees will pose the same problem, but their flowers can be sprayed with a special chemical preparation that prevents the formation of fruit.

To have shade, you do not necessarily need to plant a single large shade tree. You can plant a little grove of three or four smaller trees just west and southwest of the spot to be shaded. Such a planting will screen a relatively large area from the late-afternoon sun even if the trees are no more than 15 feet tall. If you use ornamental trees like dogwoods, flowering crab apples, Amur maples, redbuds,

FREE LANDSCAPING AIDS

County agricultural agents, long friends of the farmer, also stand ready to help homeowners with gardening problems. Their services include such basics as analyzing soil acidity and giving advice on spotty lawns, but they will often provide help in landscaping as well. In heavily populated suburban areas, agricultural extension services sponsored by federal or state agencies offer everything from demonstration of the use of mulches and the care of shrubs and trees to group tours, guided by experts, to observe well-landscaped properties and the proper use of plant materials. Some give correspondence courses in landscape design; others hold evening lecture workshops for new homeowners. Most of these services are available free or at nominal cost.

golden-rain trees, silk trees or Oriental cherries you will get a bonus of flowers in spring or summer and in some cases fruit in the fall—and a small scale compatible with a suburban house.

SUNBREAKERS AND SUN TRAPS

Trees, of course, are not the only way to provide a sitting space with shade or to keep the sun off windows and walls. Instant shade for a terrace can be provided by several kinds of rooflike shelters, from structures of thin wooden slats that filter the sun to louvers of close-set, angled boards that let in the sun in the morning but block it on summer afternoons. One of the pleasantest kinds of terrace roofs I know is one made of an "egg-crate" grid of lumber spaced to give open two- or three-foot squares. By itself, it does not offer much shade, but training a fast-growing vine—wisteria, grape, Virginia creeper—over such a structure can add greatly to the usefulness of the terrace underneath. The vine provides shade all summer while allowing a free circulation of air. If the vines are deciduous, they will shed their leaves in winter, allowing sunshine to pour through to warm the terrace for comfortable sitting even on chill fall or spring days. And if the terrace is left open to the south but sheltered on the other three sides—by house walls, solid fencing or thick evergreens—it can act as a shielded "sun trap" that will be usable still earlier and later in the year. The low winter sun, pouring in from the south, will keep such nooks pleasantly warm for sitting out and enjoying the sun in March or November. Moreover, a plant bed or some flowerpots set out there can provide a little "surprise" garden—a place where the early bulbs of spring will flower weeks before they do elsewhere in the yard.

THE FINISHING TOUCHES

There are many other ways to extend the enjoyment of your outdoor family room. Just as many indoor family rooms have a fireplace that can be used for cooking steaks, many a terrace will have its grill, either a portable metal one or a more permanent built-in structure. Some families I know, particularly in California and the Northwest, get a great deal of enjoyment out of a fire pit, a low circle of stones or firebrick built into the floor of the terrace and filled with crushed rock as a base for charcoal or wood *(page 57)*. After the hamburgers or lamb or steaks are done, family and friends can cluster around the glowing pit and enjoy the fire and conversation even when the evenings turn quite cool.

Another excellent way to get more pleasure out of your outdoor room is to light it at night. While a standard sealed-beam floodlight or two mounted on a corner of the house will suffice for some homeowners, the light cast is apt to be harsh and the source itself is blinding if you happen to look up. The best garden lighting is like good stage lighting: the sources are not obvious. Furthermore, if you place the lights away from the house instead of on it, you can create a great feeling of space even in the smallest garden, for example, by emphasizing a clump of white-trunked birch trees toward the back of the lot with a fixture concealed at its base to illuminate the trunks and leaves, or by downlighting a bed of petunias from a "mushroom" fixture on a short pipe stuck into the ground.

The best way to light a garden is to experiment until you find the right combination of lights and locations to provide the effects you want. Rather than invest right away in a complex and fixed system of underground cables, you might consider low-voltage (12-volt) lighting equipment, which is easier for the average do-it-yourselfer to work with. Low-voltage gear is often sold in a kit that includes a transformer for connecting to a house outlet, a half-dozen lights on spike standards that can be jabbed anywhere into the ground, and 100 feet or more of waterproof cord that can be snaked out and concealed behind flowers and shrubs (when the arrangement seems final, you can bury the cord in a shallow trench).

GARDEN POOLS

One of the nicest finishing touches in any outdoor room can be provided by the decorative use of water, even if it is something as simple as a stone basin set out to attract the birds. Water brings a garden alive with its reflections, its sparkling movement and soothing sound; it makes a hot day seem cooler, and if sprayed into the air can actually reduce the temperature in its vicinity by evaporation. Submersible electrical pumps, no bigger than a man's fist, that recirculate the same water over and over without the need of costly pipe connections to house plumbing make fountains a relatively inexpensive proposition these days.

A decorative garden pool need not be a large-scale affair of poured concrete, with the expense and maintenance chores that entails. There are, for example, prefabricated pool liners of rigid, earth-colored fiber glass in different shapes and sizes that can be set directly in the ground. But even this is not necessary if all you want is the feeling of water near the terrace; you can build a small garden pool in the form of a container set aboveground. This kind of pool requires no excavation; being raised, it reduces the danger that a child might fall in; and if it is made of light enough materials it can be moved about and cleaned simply by tilting it over so the water spills out. One of the simplest and most ingenious pools of this kind I have seen is one that resembles a raised plant bed. It is about four feet on a side, made of redwood planks, with a waterproof liner and a board around the top wide enough to sit on. It is the conversation piece of its owner's garden, used by adults as a bench, by children as a miniature pond for toy boats, and by both grownups and kids just to look at and dabble their fingers in.

Landscapes to live in

The most spectacular development to occur in American landscaping gained its first real momentum in the late '30s, when a group of young Harvard graduate students in landscape design—among them Garrett Eckbo, James Rose, Dan Kiley and Lawrence Halprin—rebelled against tradition and embraced ideas that were already budding in California, where the pioneering landscape architect Thomas Church had advanced them a few years earlier. They refused to view the spaces around houses simply as leftover areas in which to display plants, but as highly usable spaces for outdoor activities, for informal entertaining, or for just sitting and enjoying the sun. And so the concept of "outdoor living" gradually emerged, spurred on by the decreasing size of houses and by the development of a modern architecture that tried increasingly to relate houses to the natural landscape.

Today the results of that revolution are evident not only all over California, but from Michigan to Texas and from New Hampshire to Oregon as well. The styles and materials used vary widely from region to region, of course, but the underlying goals, and the design principles used to achieve them, are strikingly the same. With minor changes, the entrance garden shown on pages 40-41 would be as attractive and useful in Florida or Long Island as it is in Dallas. The solutions to parking problems pictured on pages 42-43 could be adapted anywhere. The same applies to other problems that by now are virtually universal: creating indoor and outdoor living rooms and dining areas with pleasant views; making play yards, service areas and garden work centers both functional and nice to look at; lighting gardens so that they are beautiful at night as well as during the day.

Not all home landscapes can be, or need be, as lush and gorgeous as the one at right, an extensively remodeled farmhouse whose owners installed a pond, summerhouse and plantings with the help of a landscape architect and contractor and a team of workmen. But with a little thought and imagination, any lot can become a landscape to live in and enjoy.

From a house in Orange, Virginia, steps invite a stroll down to a flower-adorned pond beside a summerhouse.

An inviting entrance

From under the sheltering roof the entrance
appears as a private garden, with the pastels of
a Tennessee flagstone walk, bordered by mondo
grass, leading toward the streetside wall. The
shrubs at right are American holly; at left, white
stones are used as a setting for a live oak.

In the realm of landscaping, the front yard enjoys special status—and poses special problems. While projecting a sense of individuality, it must remain in harmony with the other front yards on the street. While maintaining a dressed-up appearance, it must accommodate such practical elements as a front walk, a driveway and a mailbox. It should look neat and trim at all times and seasons, but without requiring constant attention, and it should offer a warm welcome to visitors, yet provide a sense of privacy for the owners.

How well these many, and often conflicting, goals can be achieved is demonstrated by this house in Dallas, Texas. A gracefully curving wall of old brick *(below, right)*, just high enough to screen out traffic on the street, combines with a flagstone walk to in-

vite the visitor through a garden of graceful trees, textured ground covers and other plants. The view outward from the house *(below, left)* has been endowed with equal appeal: framed by an extended roof (which protects visitors from rain and the heat of the sun), it looks toward the walled garden that appears to keep out the world.

Among the practical needs the front yard must serve are the ever-present and space-consuming demands of the automobile. For this house, off-street parking bays are convenient and unobtrusive just beyond one curve of the brick wall *(below, right)*. But homeowners in other parts of the country have found a variety of ways that driveway and parking space can be provided, conveniently and attractively, without disfiguring the front yard *(overleaf)*.

Seen from the parking area off the street, the front wall splays open to receive visitors without forgoing privacy and without need for a gate. A wax privet hedge stands in front of the wall at left. Low lighting to lead the way into the garden is provided by the hooded fixture at right.

Pleasing solutions to the parking problem

A small (20 by 42 feet) garden in back of an old Boston town house provides parking space (background) accessible from a rear alley and presents a welcoming countenance to visitors. Although the parking space crowds hard on the patio, it seems unobtrusive because it is set two feet lower and has a wrought-iron screen, as well as two small crab-apple trees and a sculpture fountain to mask its presence.

To gain guest parking and access to the garage at the back of a long, narrow lot, homeowners in Baton Rouge, Louisiana, installed a generous turnaround. This solution presented its own problem: a flat expanse of concrete. So earth was shaped into a grassy mound at the center, and a sculptural composition was created by the addition of a pebbled concrete strip and a tallow tree set in an oval of wood-bark mulch.

In another Baton Rouge house, the only access is up the driveway to dead-end parking on the apron of the garage, whose interior is the first thing visitors see. But that view is an attractive one of a blooming garden, for one side wall of the garage has been torn out and replaced by sliding glass panels; the garden itself seems to start inside the garage with a cheerful display of pots of hibiscus, croton and bird-of-paradise.

The small front yard of a San Francisco town house serves both as an entry and as a driveway to the garage. But it is not a monotonous blank surface. The designer divided the yard into diagonal sections of brick and concrete, and evergreen heaths and dwarf pine separate the footpath at left from driveway parking for guests. Privacy is provided by lily-of-the-valley trees (right) and evergreen pear trees (left).

A large native oak, its trunk nearly covered with English ivy, became the centerpiece of an ample turnaround and parking area in front of a house in Lake Oswego, Oregon. A grouping of large rhododendrons at the corner of the house serves as a second point of interest; to the left the carport roof extends over the main entrance, and to the right an azalea-bordered path leads to a terrace overlooking the lake.

The open side of a carport in Reidsville, North Carolina, marred the view from the street and the approach to the house. But rather than construct a wall or plant vines, the owners commissioned a bold modern mural to serve as a screen. The abstract design and bright colors of the painting sound a lively note of welcome to a small entry garden that is planted with azalea bushes and tall, feathery-leaved bamboo.

Outdoor living rooms

A mark of good landscaping is not only a house that invites you in, but a garden that invites you out. To be truly inviting, a garden must be an attractive and usable space for outdoor living, and it should also be a harmonious extension of the living space inside. How well this can be achieved is illustrated in the enchanting example at right, in which the garden enhances and enlarges the interior living room and itself constitutes an exterior one. The two seem to flow quite naturally together through the wide expanse of floor-to-ceiling glass, and the boundary between the two is further blurred by the continuation into the outdoors of both the tile flooring and the ceiling design; at the same time these extensions shelter the window from sun and rain and provide a narrow outdoor walk and a place to set out potted plants.

Just as the interior has been extended into the garden the outdoors has been brought inside. A row of skylights *(upper left)* provides natural overhead illumination and a tall monstera in one corner makes a bit of a garden just inside the glass. The simple, uncluttered character of the interior is mirrored in the neat plantings outside, which include the rich pile of St. Augustine grass and terraced plantings of vines and flowers against brick walls.

Thoughtfully planned, outdoor living rooms can achieve other results as well: screen out unattractive views, enhance good views, create views where none exist; solve such common problems as poor soil, blazing sun and hilly terrain; and turn even the tiniest city back yards into delightful places in which you can sit and enjoy a private outdoor world.

The San Antonio garden at right is small but its uses are many. Viewed from within the house it is an attractive extension of the living room; out of doors it offers a place to sit and a place to stroll. It also provides a deftly gentle transition from the house to the rear of the property. The steps visible at the far right lead to a grove of trees, and the way is brightened by a terraced garden of marigolds, fig vines and fatshedera growing on retaining walls of Mexican brick. A higher wall along the property line in the background is made of pierced masonry. It affords privacy, while allowing the passage of light and air and creating an interesting pattern behind the trees.

Creating and enhancing garden views

Set back on a small corner lot, a house in Ann Arbor, Michigan, looked out only on its neighbors and the street. To screen out sight and sound an 8-foot-high wall of old brick was erected in a U shape around a new deck and screened porch built out toward the side from the kitchen. Space was left between the wall and the deck for a private view: a narrow garden decorated by a crab-apple tree and climbing euonymus. The walk in the foreground, made of mottled brick, leads to the back door of the house.

A view within a forest was created for this South Dartmouth, Massachusetts, house, which was nearly surrounded by trees and evergreen shrubs. Against the woodsy backdrop is a garden with paving of concentric brick. The terrace, entered from the front walk (foreground), is bordered by shade-tolerant wax begonias and impatiens in pots and tubs. These containers can easily be moved around and taken inside the house during the winter. Tall accents are provided by Japanese white pines in wooden tubs.

A spectacular view of Buzzard's Bay and a magnificent old pear
tree were the prized back-yard assets of a 17th Century farmhouse
in South Dartmouth, Massachusetts. Capitalizing on both, a terrace
of brick laid in concentric circles and a bed of ajuga around the
tree provide an attractive place to relax and enjoy the view, and a
new door to the terrace makes the view readily accessible.

Outdoor living on problem sites

Hard clay soil in a La Jolla, California, garden defied many plants to grow. So the owners surfaced most of their patio with flagstone and sturdy, shallow-rooted dichondra. Larger plants live in containers: potted fuchsias on the ground, fibrous begonias and donkey-tail sedum in hanging baskets.

The Woodside, California, garden at right suffered mainly from too much sun. An overhanging arbor roof thick with wisteria now provides shade for an outdoor dining area and the house windows; for easy maintenance the patio is largely paved in brick, with raised bed and containers for plants.

Built on the hilly terrain of West Campton, New Hampshire, this house was nicely linked to its difficult site by a multilevel rock garden. From the door at upper left, paths and terraces lead to a lawn through granite boulders and plantings of rhododendron, juniper and laurel.

The problem of limited city space was solved
in three San Francisco back-yard gardens that
are identical in size (17 by 42 feet)—and as
different as the needs they were designed to fill.
The one at left combines flagstone and brick
with border plantings in a formal, symmetrical
pattern that makes a pleasing picture from inside
as well as out. The garden at center provides
ample space for informal entertaining with
redwood seating around a gravel court, which is
set below a curving garden walk. The garden at
right is a lively, highly personal collection of
decorative elements, including an octagonal
wood platform for lounging in the sunshine and
a path up steps of railroad ties leading to a tall,
airy gazebo set in a mass of foliage and flowers.

A garden's other lives

A small private patio opens up a kitchen in San Antonio and makes a pleasant place for outdoor meals. Floored in Mexican tile and adorned with banana plants, the patio also serves as a place to sun-bathe house plants atop a low brick wall.

"It would be nice (in a sense) if architects could design a garden without people," writes the early exponent of the landscape-to-live-in concept, Thomas Church, in his book *Your Private World*. "All kinds of lovely formal effects would be possible and every corner of the yard could be used to maximum advantage. Then, presumably, people could stand on a small platform somewhere and admire it. But gardens are for people—for people to live in and work around as well as for them to gaze at, and all designing should take this into account. There is no reason for anyone to tiptoe around his garden as if it were a Ming Dynasty vase."

Living in a garden means eating in it or near it, and designs like those shown below permit dining in pleasant surroundings, just a step away from the

kitchen stove. But eating leaves garbage, garbage needs garbage cans and garbage cans have to be stored. People wear clothes, clothes must be washed and washed clothes require clotheslines at least occasionally, despite mechanical dryers. People have children and children require places to play and places to keep their bicycles and other outdoor toys. All these paraphernalia—garbage cans, clotheslines, play equipment for children—contribute far more utility than glamor to the surroundings of a house. Yet they need not create eyesores: they can be concealed by thoughtful design and in some cases made every bit as attractive as the main garden. Such solutions illustrate how landscaping can serve the requirements of daily life, providing a maximum of usefulness and more than a modicum of beauty.

For air-conditioned indoor dining with an outdoor view, a kitchen nook in Baton Rouge looks out on a small court, where the trunk of a pecan tree is girdled by a redwood deck. An airy tropical effect is provided by hanging baskets of spider plants, gourds and English ivy; at deck level are pots of chrysanthemums (left) and Japanese fatsia (right).

Places where children can be seen and heard

In a San Antonio back yard, where the land sloped sharply, a retaining wall was required. The wall, made of Mexican brick with square tiles, was designed to do double duty, enclosing a circular sand pit in which children could play and separating it from two levels of lawn. Like all the play areas shown here, it is located so that the children can be supervised by their mother while she is at work in the house.

This Seattle back yard was transformed from a miniature swamp into a children's delight. Unwanted trees were cleared, and fir trees and redwoods (right) were planted to screen the area from the neighbors' yard. The raised deck in the background, sometimes reserved for sitting and dining, is easily converted to a badminton court; sand around the swing reduces scraped knees and yearly bills for grass seed.

In Pasadena, two children and their father built a two-level tree house in a Carob tree and painted it to blend in with the bark. The tree well beneath, which contains both potted chrysanthemums and camellias interspersed with ferns, frames the tree and covers an area that could not be planted because the tree's shallow roots were in the way. A hooded fixture hanging from the tree lights the area at night.

Fire pits are popular in Portland, Oregon, where their radiated warmth extends the use of patios on chill evenings. Around this one, seating is provided by upturned logs and a semicircular bench of cedar slats. A two-piece hinged screen can be moved about to deflect wind and reflect heat toward the marshmallow toasters. Pebbled concrete was placed around the pit and a mulch of bark and leaves on the ground beyond.

Transforming unsightly service areas

For a large family in Oregon, the necessities of life included four garbage cans as well as an assortment of children's bicycles. To screen all this equipment from the street, space outside the kitchen was enclosed by a U-shaped fence made of cedar boards, left unpainted to weather to a soft gray. Sunken receptacles topped by hinged panels were installed for two of the cans, a covered shelter built for the other two.

For another large family, in Massachusetts, the only place available for a drying yard was to one side of the garage. A section of split paling fence and a clump of Japanese black pines hide the clothesline from the street and also shelter a small garden from the prevailing wind, allowing flowers to bloom late into the year. Seedlings from the greenhouse are set out in this sheltered spot to adjust gradually to the outdoor climate.

A narrow, unused space between the garage and garden wall of a home in Pasadena, California, was converted into a lath house with a latticed roof and an easily washed-down floor of concrete. The latticework allows ample circulation of air, but at the same time it filters the hot sun and tempers the glare, creating the conditions needed for growing young plants in pots, repotting larger plants and allowing scraggly ones to revive.

In a back yard in the Georgetown section of Washington, D.C., spring bulbs in pots brighten the terrace for a while but become unsightly after their flowers have faded. The pots are then removed to the back of the yard behind a low hedge of Japanese yew and buried in a bed of wood chips, which keep the plants cool and moist the rest of the year. When they start to bloom the next spring, they are put back on the terrace.

The magic of light

Outside a Pasadena living room, a small pool mirrors the patterns of Boston ivy against a lighted wall. A low, upturned white floodlight is concealed behind a tobira bush at left; another light is affixed to the eaves of the house to create the effect of soft moonlight.

A garden softly aglow at night can seem as romantic as a love song in a birch-bark canoe. But lighting offers practical advantages as well. Since the illumined garden differs magically from its daytime self, you get two gardens for virtually the price of one. Moreover, it lengthens the hours in which the garden may be enjoyed, and expands the area available for entertaining by attracting guests out of doors. Outdoor lighting possesses, too, a virtue that is not always considered: it can do away with black windows mirroring a room's lighted interior and can even eliminate the need for shades or curtains, for it creates a view while extending the apparent size of the house at night. With newly developed equipment, garden lighting can now be installed easily at little expense.

In another part of the garden shown at left, a free-form pool is bordered by a brick wall and azalea, hibiscus and plum shrubs; it is illuminated by a yellow floodlight attached to the house and a white floodlight concealed behind shrubbery out of the picture at right.

A welcoming front yard 3

The idea of the front yard is relatively new in history, and many Americans still seem unsure what to do with it. Front yards as we know them were virtually unknown in ancient times, when the only outdoor space associated with a house was a garden enclosed within the walls or courtyard of the house itself. The notion of landscaped spaces in front of houses, at least in this country, seems to have sprung from two quite different sources: on the one hand the grand entrance gardens of European mansions, designed to impress visitors, and on the other hand the very simple greensward of colonial New England towns—the open commons on which sheep or cattle grazed, and toward which the houses and churches faced. These two ideas of ostentation and openness merged in the Victorian houses of grandfather's time—flamboyant gingerbread concoctions with front porches grandly raised behind flights of steps, where the master of the house could sit in his rocker, look out on the world going by and contemplate what a solid fellow he was.

From those days have come some landscaping notions that, like old dreams, die hard. One is the old-fashioned central walk up to the front door. In most modern suburbs hardly anyone strolls by and walks up from the street for a friendly visit anymore. The central greensward and the old elm-lined streets of the horse-and-buggy era have been replaced by traffic-filled roadways, and today everyone from guests to deliverymen pulls into the driveway by car. But the central walk has somehow survived, even though often all it does is bisect the front yard, making it look smaller and narrower than it actually is.

A far more troublesome anachronism is the old notion of "foundation planting." Plants set directly against the house performed a function of sorts in the old days: the meticulously sheared shrubs not only added to the house's impressive effect, but they also hid its ungainly foundations, green latticework and basement windows. For today's lower, porchless houses, however, foundation plantings—if needed at all—must be used in a more informal man-

At dusk an entrance patio in Pasadena, California, provides an open-armed welcome. Beneath the sheltering branches of an old olive tree are lush beds of Hahn's ivy and low walls fronted by white azaleas.

ner to avoid looking like a row of nursery specimens drawn up on parade, or, as the plants grow, a rising sea of spinach gradually obscuring the windows and engulfing the house.

AN OUTDOOR ENTRANCE HALL   Old-fashioned patterns like these generally look wrong today simply because the purposes they once served no longer exist. As living styles have changed so have the functions of the front yard and the demands placed on its plants, shrubs and walks. Today it is expected to satisfy a number of different, often conflicting, needs. It must, as always, look attractive to passersby, enhancing the house and expressing its owner's personality. It must also perform some very practical tasks. Careful planning of the landscape can help visitors drive in, park and walk directly to the front door without brushing by or stumbling into overgrown or misplaced shrubs—and without blundering in confusion to a side or kitchen door.

When esthetics and practicality are nicely balanced, the space in front acts as a kind of outdoor entrance hall, a semipublic area that greets visitors and leads them through a graceful transitional stage from the busy world of the street to the private world inside. Some of the best-designed front yards I have seen carry this idea of the outdoor entrance hall a step further. There the space near the front door becomes a jewel-like garden that can be enjoyed from both inside and outside the house. Such landscaping makes a home that not only brings pride and pleasure to its owner but is comfortable to use and a delight to the entire neighborhood.

PLANNING FOR ACCESS   To achieve the goal of a convenient, inviting and attractive entryway to your property, it pays to think about functions first and specific plants and materials later. The primary function of the front of the house is access: it is, after all, where you go in and come out. Your freedom in laying out these access routes may be severely limited, since their arrangement is largely dictated by factors you cannot control—lot size, house and street relationships, boundary lines. But careful attention to the details of planning drives and walks can bring big dividends of utility and attractiveness.

Most homeowners need a driveway that not only leads to house and garage but also allows for off-street parking. The entrance to this driveway should be wide enough to allow a car to swing in easily. To eliminate the hazards of backing out again, particularly into a busy street, it is desirable that the driveway incorporate some sort of turnaround space. Not all homeowners can afford the space or expense of a semicircular driveway providing a separate entrance and exit, but it is almost always feasible to provide a simple backaround—a driveway appendage into which a car can swing while reversing direction. The backaround also serves as a parking bay for extra cars (*below*). It need not be paved in the same material as the driveway itself; any material that will drain well and support the weight of a car—compacted gravel or bricks laid in sand over a coarse rock base—will stand up to the backaround's lighter use. It should be provided with a bumper strip —a curb of brick, stone or a length of timber—to keep cars from overrunning plantings. Tall plants should be located at least 5 feet beyond this strip to allow for the car's front overhang.

So that both family and guests can get from car to front door without tripping over bushes or stepping onto wet grass, there should be enough room beside parked cars for a walk 3 to 4 feet wide along one edge of the driveway (*page 76*). This strip is simply a more convenient version of the old center walk, located where people will use it; if made of a material different from the driveway it will be recognized as a walk and will also act as a guideline for them as they drive in, particularly at night.

The main path leading from the driveway to the front door should be at least 4 feet wide to allow two people to walk side by side instead of trooping Indian file. If the path involves steps, their treads should be deeper in relation to their height than inside stairs for safety and comfort. Even on steep grades the treads should be at least 12 inches deep and the risers no higher than 6 inches. If

TURNAROUNDS, PASSAROUNDS AND DRIVEWAY PARKING

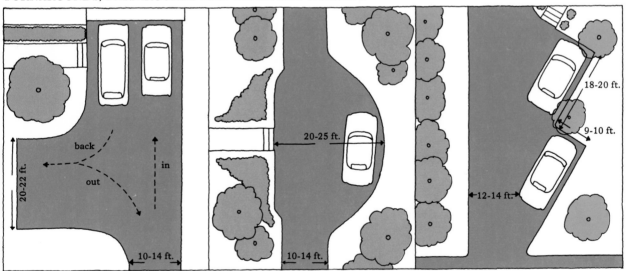

The hazards of backing a car out of a driveway can be avoided by building a Y-shaped turnaround. Cars back into the Y, then move into the street headfirst. The turnaround also provides parking for two cars.

A simple device for gaining extra parking space and preventing one car from blocking another in a driveway is to widen the driveway into a passaround; this should be as long as the length of two cars.

A "saw-tooth" arrangement allows cars to be parked at an angle. Plantings should be kept 5 feet back to prevent cars from overrunning them, with a low curb set at the head of each bay to stop the wheels.

wider treads are possible, the height of the riser should decrease —a 5-inch riser for a 15-inch tread, a 4-inch riser for an 18-inch tread, and so on. Any walkway, particularly one with steps, should be adequately lighted at night.

One further practical consideration: if you live in a region where snowfall is heavy enough so that driveways must be plowed, leave enough space for piled-up snow to be pushed off the drive and out of the way of people and traffic. Make sure that no shrubs or other woody plants are in the way; they can be severely injured by the compacted snow and the pressure of the big blade behind it.

FRONT-YARD PLANTINGS

While the layout of drives and walks depends mainly on the house plan, the design of the plantings for the front yard is limited only by imagination and taste. Utility, in the most down-to-earth sense, may take second place to esthetics. But both goals are best achieved if a few general guidelines are kept in mind.

First of all, front-yard plantings should be simple. Some landscape architects I know go so far as to say that you should place no more than three kinds of plants in front of a house, and use no fewer than three of each. This is a bit extreme, but there is no question that by limiting the number and kinds of plants you choose, and grouping several plants of the same kind together, you can achieve a feeling of unity and cohesiveness that is impossible to attain with a hodgepodge of plant varieties. Moreover, when the plants grow together, as they inevitably will, they will intermingle more harmoniously than when different kinds of plants crowd one another. The resulting simplicity will make the plantings enhance the house rather than overwhelm it.

Because front-yard space is usually limited, it is wise to choose plants that will remain small in scale and rather loose and airy in appearance—among trees, for example, one of several types of Japanese maple, which have graceful limbs and feathery foliage and are slow-growing, rather than a stiff, dense, fast-growing pyramidal Colorado spruce. The kind to stay away from are young forest trees; while these may be the cheapest and most readily available at a nursery, they can quickly outgrow their usefulness. It is not uncommon for some varieties of young pines to shoot up three or four feet a year. If planted near the house, especially near a window, it can soon rob the interior of light or become too big to remain in scale with the house. If you lop it off to keep it under control, it will be forced to grow in an unnatural shape and lose most of its native charm. (This is not to suggest, of course, that if you have a large and handsome old tree, you should cut it down. Treasure it for the feeling of shelter it gives, even it it makes your house look small in comparison.)

Shrubs, too, need to be kept in scale with the house, especially if they are to be planted fairly close to the walls. There is a wide choice among low, slow-growing plants—boxwood, Japanese holly, and the dwarf varieties of juniper, yew, rhododendron and euonymus, for instance. But unless you are willing to spend your weekends with hedge shears in hand, avoid such quick-growing plants as privet and spirea, even though they are relatively inexpensive and sturdy.

Seek out plants that thrive in your climate and soil; there is nothing so unsightly in a front yard as plants that must be wrapped up like mummies to carry them through the winter, or that turn brown from heat and dryness every summer. It is far better to have handsome specimens of common bushes than exotic but sickly shrubs. To find out which plants do well in your locality, check the encyclopedia section, Chapter 5, which keys trees and shrubs to regional conditions. It is also helpful to drive around your own neighborhood, noting which species look healthy and which do not, as well as to visit a local nurseryman who grows his own stock (rather than one who has only a sales yard and may import his plants from somewhere else). The plants that thrive in his nursery through winter and summer probably will do the same for you.

When setting out plants in the front yard, keep small shrubs

PLANTING FOR PRIVACY AND VIEWS

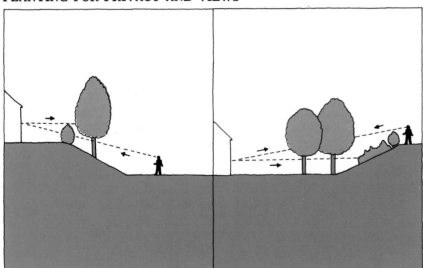

High and low plantings, combined with changes in ground level, can screen out unwanted views as well as create pleasant ones. Here a hedge blocks out passersby on the street below; trees filter cross-street views.

With the house below the street, trees are used to screen the view of the passerby and his view of the house; the slope up to the street is planted with a hedge and ground cover to provide a view from inside.

ONE TREE, THREE SHAPES

A plant's environment can make a dramatic difference in what it looks like. In the open sunlight of a back-yard garden, where it may be periodically fed and watered, a white fir will take on the fat, bushy pyramidal shape of a Christmas tree, with wide-spreading lower branches that may touch the ground, but it will rarely exceed a mature height of 50 feet. In a crowded forest where it has to compete for sunlight with its neighbors, the same tree, if it survives, may exceed 100 feet at maturity, rising on a towering, branchless lower trunk to thrust a green topknot through the forest canopy toward the sun. On a rocky mountain slope, a white fir seedling that has managed to take root may assume a still different shape. Bent by wind and stunted by drought, it may become a low and twisted plant little higher than other wild shrubs around it.

PRINCIPLES PUT TO WORK

and bushes at least 4 to 6 feet away from the house. If set closer, they may be robbed of sunlight, deprived of rain by a wide overhang or dried out by heat reflected from the wall. Separated from the house and planted in a band of some width rather than a narrow row, they add a three-dimensional effect to the landscape that makes the house seem more substantial.

To increase the sense of depth, place a major planting, such as a group of trees, a considerable distance in front of the house. To anyone approaching or passing by in a car, the trees will change position in relation to the house, giving an impression of depth and movement to the setting. The effect will be enhanced if the trees have several trunks, branches not too close to the ground and an arching shape—birch, mountain ash, hawthorn and shad-blow are all excellent for this purpose.

It is also possible to make the house seem wider than it actually is. Planting a small tree or clump of trees such as dogwood or flowering cherry near the corners will do the trick.

If you have an expanse of bare foundation wall facing the street, a problem common in split-level houses, it does not have to be concealed by a line of stiff foundation shrubbery. It may better be softened by loose, unsheared shrubs like andromeda, laurel or holly planted informally, or by one of a number of vines suited to covering masonry walls—Boston ivy, winter creeper, Virginia creeper, climbing hydrangea, creeping fig. Such vines, however, should not be allowed to climb onto wood siding or shingles because their adhesive "holdfasts" can damage the wood.

While the best all-around ground cover for most front yards is grass, other kinds of plants should be considered for particular areas; they can add interesting textures when they are planted in beds, create borders for walks and driveways, hold slopes in place, fill out shady areas where grass will not grow, and generally cut down on front-yard maintenance. Planted in beds around trees and shrubs, they can serve to unify and set off the larger plants, particularly while they are young and still spaced apart.

If simple landscaping principles like the ones above are combined and salted with a little imagination, they produce stunning results. Yet often they are ignored, and the results are disastrous.

A dreadful example of the disasters is a house I visited for the first time not long ago, to attend an evening meeting. I must admit that it was a cold, rainy night, which did not help, but I doubt I would have liked the house much better in the light of day. To begin with, I drove up and down the block twice looking for the house number (which, it turned out, was hidden by an overgrown shrub). There was no place to park or turn around in the driveway, so I left my car on the street, not sure whether I would get a ticket or not. As I walked up a narrow path to the front door, the dripping wet branches of plants placed too close to the paving brushed against my pants legs. I walked with that shuffle people adopt when they are not quite sure what they are going to trip over in the dim light from one small bulb over the front door. What I could see of the house was hardly inviting; it seemed buried behind two extremely large evergreen trees, one placed symmetrically on each side, that hid the front windows almost entirely, and a string of rather scrubby winter-burned bushes. I must say I did not enjoy the meeting very much.

Not far away, in fact in the same general neighborhood, there is a house that I enjoy going back to again and again. It is basically the same as the first one, a typical builder's model that we call a Cape Cod Colonial around my part of the country. But the owner, with a little thought, and not much more money, has made it a delight for himself and his visitors by creating a modern version of a New England dooryard garden (pages 20-21). That makes the front so distinctive he hardly needs a house number for identification. When you get out of your car in his driveway, which includes space for parking, you step onto a little landing strip of patterned brick about 15 feet long and 5 feet wide, lighted by two low fixtures. From there a 5-foot-wide walk leads to the dooryard garden, which is enclosed by a knee-high hedge of boxwood that extends in an L around to the front door. Inside the hedge is a little 10-by-15-foot entrance patio of brick. It is bordered by ivy, through which some charming and rather uncommon miniature bulbs sprout— grape hyacinths and species daffodils in the spring, garden lilies in summer, autumn-flowering crocus in the fall—all chosen not only for their color but for their small scale, in keeping with the garden itself. Between bricks here and there the owner has planted sprigs of creeping thyme, which gives off a delicious fragrance when stepped on. In one corner of the garden is a little white wrought-iron settee; it provides a place to set packages or wait, or to sit in the sun at certain times of day, but it is a nice note of welcome whether it is used or not. To give the garden vertical accents and a sense of welcoming enclosure, three cornelian cherry trees, which rarely grow more than 25 feet high, are planted. The trees shade the garden and the front windows from hot summer sun, and filter out the view of the street, even in winter when their leaves are gone; along with the rest of the dooryard garden, they also make a charming view from inside the house as well as out. As a final touch, the owner has placed on his front step a weathered clay jar planted with Alpine strawberries to be enjoyed at close range by visitors waiting at the door. With a welcome like that, who wouldn't enjoy coming back?

PLANTING FOR THE BIRDS

Not to be overlooked when choosing trees and shrubs is their potential for attracting birds, which add flashes of color and song to any landscape and are among a gardener's best allies in insect control. Birds are drawn to many plants that bear fruit, berries or seeds—crab apples, holly, honeysuckle, cherry trees, to name only a few. In northern areas, bittersweet, autumn olive and other bushes that produce berries in winter will help keep birds around. Birds also need cover to court, nest and hide in, particularly during cold weather, when they seek out protection from biting winds in evergreens such as junipers, cedars and yews. For really close observation, a feeding station and a birdbath can be used to lure birds in front of a window or beside a porch.

Using textures and patterns

While they last, bright colors certainly are the most eye-catching characteristics of a landscape, more so even than the shapes of plants and man-made structures. Frequently overlooked is the texture of things; yet it is the texture—and the patterns textures create—that determines whether a garden seems unified and harmonious or harsh and disjointed.

The other two major elements of design—color and overall form—are easier to handle since they are more apparent to the eye. But using texture effectively requires great care and discrimination. The studied juxtaposition of textures—coarse against fine, rough against smooth, shiny against dull, thin against dense, stiff against soft, sharp against rounded—can make a narrow space look wider, a shallow space deeper, a steep slope gentler; it can direct the eye away from a trouble spot or toward one of special interest, give balance to an unbalanced arrangement, provide either tranquillity or excitement, add spice to a dull area. Scale—the relationship of the size of the repeating pattern to the size of the setting—is also an important factor in the effective use of textures. In a small garden around a doorstep, a ground cover with large, widely spaced leaves might seem obtrusive and make the area seem smaller than it is. But the same bold ground cover used beneath a copse of trees at a distance from the house could provide a strong pattern, transforming separate trees into a single, powerful image.

The front-yard corner shown at right is an unusual example of virtuosity in the use of texture. The neat, bristly surface of the St. Augustine grass visually enlarges a restricted space. On the bank at the left is a crinkly bed of shiny-leaved star jasmine, a medium-sized, although lively, texture. In the bed above the wall the rough-textured English ivy makes an emphatic background, giving balance to the composition. The gradual transition from fine to medium to coarse texture leads the eye in a sinuous path from one area to the next—and the slope is made to seem so gentle that it is hard to realize the house perches half a story above the lawn.

Contrasting textures in evergreens and bricks create a pattern of muted liveliness for a house in San Antonio.

Fig vine on a stucco wall

Brick wall with sword ferns

Sempervivum and rock

A palette of textures

If textures' influences on a landscape are subtle, they are without limit. The range of effects is so astonishingly broad because the variety among textures, although not obvious at first glance, is seen to be great from a close look at the surfaces around house and garden. Then it becomes clear how extensive is the difference in character between a stone and a wooden wall; between the smooth domesticated appearance of a close-cropped lawn and the wild ephemeral quality of uncut grasses moving in the breeze; between the hard, glossy finish of rhododendron leaves and the soft mounds of a shaded, mossy bank.

Such differences in textures are exploited by contrasting one against the other. The faint roughness of the stucco wall at top left, for example, is emphasized by the sharp zigzag of a fig vine's leaves. In a similar fashion the irregular form of sword ferns enhances the order of bricks *(center, left),* and the rounded lobes of English ivy make the most of the vertical lines in cedar boards *(center, right).* More subtle contrasts can be equally effective, as when feathery juniper is backed by the coarser texture of mondo grass *(bottom, far right).* It is even possible to create a contrast of textures with a single material such as stone *(bottom, right);* one part of the overall pattern comes from the outlines of the stones, the other from their surfaces.

The examples pictured here are an arbitrary selection from gardens around the country. But even these few samples make clear that, as a rule, nature ungroomed has a rough hide. Large smooth surfaces, like regular outlines, are not frequently found. That is why a straight, slick concrete walk might seem out of character in a woodsy setting, while a winding gravel path would look more at home. But that is also why an exception to the rule—the mirror face of a still pond, for instance—stands out so strongly in its green frame as a delightful surprise.

Coarse sand, river stones, granite rock

Autumn maple leaves

Cedar fence with English ivy

Yaupon holly trunks and ground ivy

Wall of quarried fieldstone

Juniper over mondo grass

Composing with textures: two styles

A spectrum of textures has been used in this garden, a seemingly wild woodland glen that is actually contained in a narrow yard in Dallas, Texas. The smooth, soft evergreen ground ivy at the right (shown close up on the preceding page) makes a quiet setting for the slim gray trunks of yaupon holly. It is marked off by the strong line of a path of fine, crunchy river sand from the border of coarse textures (left) that creates an exciting feeling of rhythmic motion—spiky mondo grass next to the path, liriope with its lily-shaped leaves, Formosa azalea and, in the background, the graceful fronds of wood ferns.

Contrasting with the exuberant use of texture in the
picture at the left is the carefully regimented pattern of
this composition in New Orleans. The shrubs—elaeagnus,
dwarf azalea, dwarf yaupon, variegated euonymus and
barberry—have been pruned into isolated mounds to
emphasize texture rather than natural form, creating
solid silhouettes that stand out against the background
surfaces of raked sand, rough concrete and wood fencing.
The balanced repetition of textured mounds gives the
harmony expected of a formal pattern, yet the plants are
not so uniformly placed that the design is monotonous.

Texture and pattern to walk on

This hillside bed of English ivy in Ann Arbor, Michigan, would seem mushy and shapeless were it not for the strong, repetitive pattern of the concrete rounds that create a graceful winding stairway. The ivy, shade-tolerant and evergreen, anchors the soil on the steep bank. The coarse texture of its leaves is appropriate to an area of this size and, when it is combined with a dominating architectural feature like this stairway, it provides the strong form that a large plant bed requires.

A heavy, blank expanse of asphalt driveway (left) is handsomely accented in this Virginia front yard by the pronounced texture of a flanking walkway of rough-cut stone slabs and treated oak beams. Besides providing a dry place to alight from a car, the walk makes an attractive border for the holly bushes at the right and fills the need for dramatic distinction between the nontexture of asphalt and the soft, small-scaled texture of the pine-bark mulch underlying the holly bushes.

To reach an elevated teahouse in this hilly garden in Southern California, a leisurely approach was laid out on a ramp rather than a stairway. Adding interest to the starkly geometric design is a medley of woody textures —rough-cut boards edging the walk and steps of cross-sectioned tree trunks set in a deep mulch of shredded fir bark. The central, triangular panel has been planted with variegated English ivy, surrounding a shaded electric lantern that provides illumination at night.

A harmonious blend of texture, pattern and color flows through this garden in Charlottesville, Virginia. The voluptuous plantings—a curved border of bronze-colored ajuga topped by the rounded forms of boxwood, azaleas in bloom, and masses of sweet alyssum and white and purple pansies—create a sea of velvet. Through it as a foil runs the geometric herringbone pattern of a walk of weathered brick, adding a counterpoint of angularity and helping create a solid axis for balance.

Stone, laid in a bold pattern, parts a billowy
sea of needled evergreens for an elegant
—and relatively carefree—entrance to a
seaside house in Byram, Connecticut. The
deceptively simple composition changes
color subtly over the seasons as the trees
and shrubs dim and brighten their shades of
green. But it gets its impact from texture
—the contrasts among the plants (shore,
Sargent and Andorra juniper, backed by the
taller Japanese black and red pines).

Places for work and play 4

Not everything that must be fitted into a garden is beautiful. In fact, the more beautiful the garden, the more certain you can be that there is a large inventory of mowers, rakes, hoes, wheelbarrows and bags of fertilizer hidden away somewhere. There will also be trash cans, perhaps a pile of firewood and a compost heap. And if there are children, there will be toys—tricycles and wagons, swings and slides.

What do you do with all that stuff? One of my neighbors segregates it and conceals it. Outside his kitchen door he has a kitchen garden, partially floored in brick and screened from view by a high fence; it contains a storage cabinet for the garbage cans, stacked logs, and several rows of vegetables and herbs. Back of the garage a tall evergreen hedge hides another area for a permanently strung clothesline, a tool shed and a compost pile. To one side of the lot, screened by a row of forsythia bushes, is the children's play yard. My neighbor has given up yelling at them to pick up their junk; if he can't see the clutter of toys and other play equipment from the house or terrace, he doesn't worry about it.

Another neighbor of mine takes a different point of view. He wants to see his whole lot, not make it seem smaller by chopping it up into neat compartments. He makes space for his trash cans and garden tools in the garage. When his wife wants to dry sheets or air clothing, she pulls a temporary clothesline from a reel attached to the side of the house and fastens it to a tree. The children's swings and seesaw, brightly painted, stand exposed at the back of the yard so the kids can be seen at play. The vegetable garden, too, is open to view; its owner likes to look at the rows of lettuce, corn and carrots he grows so well. He has simply indicated the boundary between the vegetable garden and the lawn with a row of blueberry bushes. Every year the bushes give him decorative white flowers in the spring, bright red foliage in the autumn, and (if he covers them with cheesecloth to keep the birds off) enough berries to make a dozen or so pints of delicious jam.

Off the terrace of an Ann Arbor, Michigan, home, a youthful member of a family of golf enthusiasts blasts out of a homemade sand trap—a decorative garden element that can also serve as a sand pile for children.

Which of my neighbors is right? Both are, of course, since each enjoys his garden tremendously. Each simply uses landscaping differently to achieve goals important to him.

PLAY YARDS

Both, like everyone with growing children, need to provide a certain amount of play space and play equipment. An area close to a kitchen or living-room window permits Mother to keep an eye on small children. An elaborate enclosure is not necessary; you can create an oversized play pen right on the lawn by setting out an inexpensive temporary enclosure—so-called snow fencing, made of narrow wood slats and wire, is quite adequate. Grass makes an ideal floor for such a pen, since a toddler is unlikely to skin a knee or an elbow tumbling on it. When the fencing is removed, rolled up and put away, the lawn can be used for something else.

As children get their first wheeled toys, the advantages of a relatively smooth, hard surface become apparent. If you have a paved terrace *(Chapter 2),* it will be easier to keep small children and their tricycles there, away from the hazards of the driveway and street. A garden path, such as one of hard-packed gravel, also extends the range of the three-wheeler set. If such a path is laid out around one or more sides of the lawn, it also separates the grass areas from the plant beds and acts as a "mowing strip"—one wheel of the lawn mower can run on the path, eliminating any possibility of damaging plants that overhang their beds and doing away with the tedious chore of hand trimming the edge of the lawn.

One of the universal joys of early childhood is the sandbox. It can be literally that—a box bought from a store or built of 1-by-8-inch boards and filled with the clean play sand sold for this purpose (ordinary builder's sand is cheaper, if a little scratchier, and perfectly adequate). If the sides of the sandbox are built of fairly heavy materials—2-by-10-inch planks, squared logs or even brick—and located with an eye to future use, the structure can be converted later into a raised planting bed.

As children start to outgrow sandboxes and tricycles and go in for more active play, parents begin to think about such things as swings and slides and seesaws. You needn't rush out to buy the most expensive set at the department store. If the play area has a tree large enough to support the weight, hang an old tire at the end of a heavy rope (with holes punched in the bottom of the tire to let rain water drain out); this is still one of the best and safest pieces of play equipment ever devised. Another perfectly good homemade rig is a simple slide made of a 2-by-8-foot piece of tempered hardboard set on a slope and given a coat of household wax.

Wherever play equipment like a swing set or a jungle gym is located, it should be anchored solidly by setting the legs in con-

SURFACING A PLAY AREA

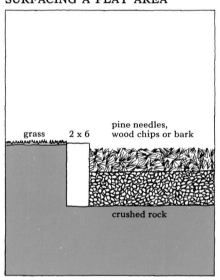

grass   2 x 6   pine needles, wood chips or bark

crushed rock

Beneath a swing or climbing apparatus in a play yard, a resilient, self-draining bed of pine needles, wood chips or shredded bark can be used to cushion falls and eliminate the problem of worn-away grass. The area should first be excavated to a depth of 5 or 6 inches; then lay down 2 or 3 inches of coarse gravel or crushed rock and top with 2 inches of needles, bark or chips. Around the sides 2-by-6-inch boards, set on edge at soil level to make mowing easier, help keep the material where it belongs.

crete, and provided with a resilient surface underneath to absorb the shock of the inevitable falls. Again, a good grade of grass is satisfactory if the play equipment does not get extraordinarily heavy use. (It is a good idea to avoid seed mixtures containing clover, since the flowers will attract stinging insects.)

But grass tends to wear away in critical spots, which become muddy potholes following a rainstorm; moreover, grass usually stays damp for a good hour or two after a rain. Other choices avoid that problem but may be messier. A ground cover of pine needles, purchased at a garden supply center or gathered in a pinewoods, is soft, has a pleasant smell, dries quickly and interlocks to stay in place. Equally resilient and fast-drying are the many varieties of shredded tree bark and wood chips that can be bought as mulch at garden stores. Another durable, if slightly more abrasive, surface can be made of the common sandy gravel used by building contractors. Such sandy gravel is readily available; the particles of different size interlock, giving a reasonably stable and resilient surface that is less likely than sand or gravel alone to get kicked out onto the surrounding grass. Before placing any of these loose surfacing materials, it is a good idea to excavate the play area to a depth of 5 or 6 inches and put in 2 or 3 inches of coarse gravel, particularly if your soil does not drain quickly. A curb of lumber—2-by-6s on edge—will help contain the material, but it should be sunk flush with the lawn to make mowing easy.

Should you decide to screen the play equipment from the rest of the yard with a hedge, tough and inexpensive plants are best. Unless you have ample space they should be of a kind that stands shearing so that you can keep them from taking up too much room, and they should be dense enough to form a visual barrier. And since children will probably bump into them, they should be relatively soft-textured—not filled with thorns like shrub roses or stubby and hard when pruned like pines and spruces. Two plants that meet all these specifications are arborvitae and privet; both can be sheared to a 2-foot thickness when space is at a premium.

As children become teenagers, the open area of lawn that is so attractive to the eye can be used for any number of activities, from a game of touch football to tether ball or croquet. Don't worry about damage to the lawn; the fun is worth the risk and if the grass is occasionally trampled it will recover quickly. Just remember that an open area of lawn should be really open to be usable; trees and specimen shrubs scattered here and there make active games difficult.

When children reach the teen years, many families start getting internal pressure for the biggest toy of all—a swimming pool in the back yard. A swimming pool is a fine thing to have, but it can dom- **SWIMMING POOLS** inate the whole landscaping scheme, especially on a small lot.

Nevertheless I have a pool, and I wouldn't be without it. Mine is a "naturalized" pool, irregular in shape and planted so closely around the edge with native plants—blueberry bushes, rose mallows, water-loving irises and purple loosestrife—that you might think it had always been there, since it looks like a woodland pond. It is simply a scooped-out hole lined with a flexible sheet of black plastic, covered with a 6-inch layer of sand that holds it in place and adds to the natural appearance.

If you contemplate putting in a pool of any kind place it, as I have, as close to one side of your property as building regulations allow in order to leave uninterrupted space on the rest of the lot. You will have less of a maintenance chore, especially with a regular concrete pool, which should look neat, if you do not place the pool near trees or shrubs, which litter the water (needled evergreens are even worse offenders than deciduous plants). I did not follow this standard—and generally sound—advice when laying out my pool, and my weeping willows drop leaves into the water. I just clean them up once in a while; it's worth the trouble.

The security fencing that many communities require around a private pool adds to the problem of landscaping. If local ordinances call for an unclimbable chain-link fence, it can be made less

SCREENS FOR THE YARD

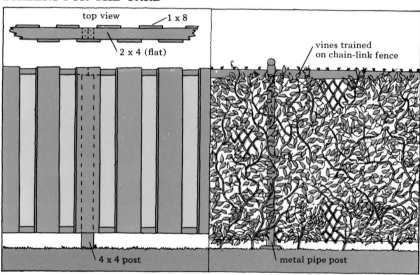

A simple fence of boards provides privacy for a service yard while letting breezes through. It is built of 4-by-4-inch posts, joined by 2-by-4s, with 1-by-8-inch boards that are nailed on in an alternating pattern.

A standard chain-link fence, held taut by pipe sections, will keep animals away from garbage cans or children from wandering into a pool. It is more attractive and gives better screening if planted with vines.

visible and objectionable if it is painted black or dark green—not a difficult job with a paint pan and roller—and planted with evergreen vines or shrubs. If the kind of security barrier is not stipulated, a variety of open and solid fencing materials can be used to break up the overall feeling of enclosure; just be careful that you do not use such a variety that your yard becomes a hodgepodge.

If a planted screen is more in keeping with your neighborhood, select plants that are sufficiently dense to deflect wind and tough enough to resist damage from it. Among the evergreens, spruces are often used for this purpose; they can be planted close enough together so the branches interlock. Deciduous plants can also be used; such species as Russian olive trees, bush honeysuckles or lilacs will provide decorative, flowering screens in summer when you are using the pool; they will drop their leaves in fall, admitting more winter sunshine, but unless they are planted far enough back from the pool, their leaves may create a litter problem. The house itself might be the visual barrier on a second side; toward a neighboring lot you can use heavy wire fencing just high enough to keep out wandering children and dogs, and hide the wire with plants that provide good coverage and good looks at the same time. Dense-leaved, fast-growing flowering vines are the best for this purpose—clematis, silverlace or wisteria, for example. A fence can also be concealed with roses—either climbing roses trained on it or tall grandifloras or shrub roses planted in front of it.

SERVICE AREAS

Decorative planting and fencing can also be used around another special-purpose space more common in back yards: the service area. Such an area can accommodate almost anything—trash, clotheslines for airing linens or drying laundry, a small boat and trailer not in use, a garden work center, even a lath house to provide filtered shade for tender young seedlings.

If you screen a service yard with plants, use evergreen varieties; they will hide any clutter the year around. A careful selection will give you a living wall that is inexpensive, dense and fast-growing, yet one that can be easily sheared to keep both height and width under control. Upright junipers, for example, will do well if planted no more than 2½ to 3 feet apart; if they are bought when they are 3 to 4 feet tall they will provide at least partial screening immediately. They can be sheared to remain at almost any height you want from 4 to 6 or 7 feet. Other good choices are upright yews, podocarpus and Japanese holly; all are densely foliaged but can be pruned to keep height and width under control.

If space is very limited, as it often is in side yards, a fence or masonry wall will leave more ground free. One of the simplest fences that will provide a visual barrier without creating a stockade effect is one of wire mesh covered with a lushly leaved, fast-growing evergreen vine such as English or Algerian ivy. An inexpensive vine that will grow beautifully on a fence and is semievergreen (it loses some but not all of its leaves in frost zones) is Hall's honeysuckle; it requires little care and bears very fragrant white flowers. But vines, even those that are evergreen, may leave gaps in inappropriate places. A more reliable, and more total, enclosure is a board fence. If you build one, keep in mind the need for ventilation within the service yard. One of the easiest ways to achieve this is with a fence of staggered boards *(page 84)* or a pierced wall of masonry blocks. The staggered design provides the bonus of an interesting shadow pattern, and can be a handsome backdrop for a border of annuals or roses.

Several flooring materials are suited to a service yard; the choice depends largely on the intensity of use. Grass is adequate if the yard is relatively large, if there is no heavy traffic back and forth that might wear a path, and if the yard is not so cut up by objects and protrusions that it would be difficult to mow. If your service area is small and heavily used, a sturdier, quick-draining surface is better: common brick laid in sand; asphalt (perhaps extended from an adjacent driveway); or crushed rock.

OUTDOOR STORAGE

If you fence in a service yard, one of the inner sides of the fence provides a ready-made back for a storage cabinet built to hold garden tools, garden supplies and yard toys. The simplest kind of cabinet to build is one about 3 feet deep, 6 feet tall and 8 feet long, with ¾-inch-thick plywood walls, roof and floor. To avoid warping and splintering, use a weather-resistant, exterior-grade plywood. Slope the roof slightly to let rain water drain off; to keep the contents dry raise the floor above the ground by setting the cabinet on concrete blocks (if any wood touches the ground, it should be treated with a preservative such as creosote or pentachlorophenol to prevent rot). A piece of leftover plywood will make a ramp so that you can wheel a lawn mower up into the cabinet without the necessity of lifting it. Inside the cabinet, nails and hooks can be used to keep tools up off the floor and out of the way of bags of fertilizer.

A GARDEN WORK CENTER

If you are a true gardener, you may go on to build a more elaborate garden work center. You can design it almost any way your special gardening interests indicate, but here are some features I have found useful:

A location near the driveway permits heavy garden materials to be transferred directly to the work center from your car, and you will avoid many a backache.

A potting bench about 2 feet wide, 4 feet long and 3 feet high is a great convenience for working, especially if it is accompanied by a tall stool that lets a weary gardener sit as he works.

A water supply saves many steps. To avoid a large plumber's bill, buy a secondhand sink with a faucet and bring water to it with a garden hose; drain the sink into a dry well—a hole in the ground filled with large stones.

An electric line to your work center not only will provide light for evening work but will enable you to use power tools or to install fluorescent lights to speed the growth of seedlings.

Heavy plastic or metal garbage cans with tight-fitting lids are excellent for storing materials that might attract mice—particularly such fertilizers as cottonseed meal and bone meal. Cans will also keep peat moss damp, making it easier and pleasanter to work with. If the containers are placed on wheel-around dollies (squares of ¾-inch plywood mounted on casters) they will be easier to move when loaded.

An especially important item that should be included in any work center is a cabinet that can be padlocked to keep poisonous garden chemicals beyond the reach of inquisitive children.

The location and design of other common garden service areas—a vegetable or cutting garden and a cold frame or hotbed to give your spring planting a head start—are dictated to a large extent by the requirements of growing plants.

The low glass- or plastic-topped structure of a cold frame or hotbed is not ugly, but it is not particularly pretty either. It is best to tuck it away out of the main view from the back of the house, perhaps shielded by a short section of hedge or fence. It must, of course, have abundant sunlight, and thus should be set on a north-south axis with the sloping top facing south.

A vegetable or cutting garden, too, needs sunlight, but not necessarily all day. My own vegetable garden is surrounded by trees on three sides, the open side being toward the south. It receives about six hours of sunlight a day, and that is plenty. Nor does a vegetable garden need to be hidden from view if you keep it reasonably neat. In my garden, after the harvest I clean up the debris and sow winter rye grass; it covers the black earth with green in a hurry. In the spring, I plow the rye under to improve the soil. Such a garden does require some attention, but once you discover the unmatched flavor of freshly picked corn, tomatoes or lettuce, you will probably decide that the effort is well spent. You may even discover that many vegetables are as attractive as any plant you grow for an ornament. They, like everything else you see around your house, are part of the landscape, able to contribute to both the beauty and the practicality of your own private environment.

"FLOATING" GARDENS

One of the landscaping wonders that the Spaniards found when they conquered the New World were the so-called floating gardens of Xochimilco, a village south of Mexico City named for the Aztec words meaning "field of flowers."

The gardens do not actually float; they only look that way. They are artificial islands built among a network of canals engineered by the Aztecs to irrigate the land. The islands were sown with food crops, chiefly maize, on which the Aztec population—an estimated 300,000 people—fed. The gardens and the canals can still be seen today, but they are only a remnant of the originals.

SPECIAL GARDENS

The stylemakers speak

Every era creates its style and every style reflects its era. Modern landscape design, mirroring the economics and the mood of its time, rejects ostentation in favor of simplicity, and formality in favor of fitness and function. In this section, some of the leading practitioners of the art voice their philosophies beside examples of their work.

But no style grows without roots. The tradition of natural simplicity that is now flowering in gardens around the country was sired, or grandsired, in the mid-19th Century by Frederick Law Olmsted, whose influence on the look of American cities has long survived him. He designed the most famous of U.S. public parks: New York's Central and Prospect Parks, Chicago's Washington and Jackson Parks, Boston's Back Bay Fens—more than 80 all told. Coining the very term "landscape architecture," he established as its principle that the terrain and natural resources of the site must dictate the planning. Olmsted's ideas were carried further by Jens Jensen, a Dane who came to the U.S. with a dime in his pocket, toiled as a parks laborer, and became a parks superintendent and world-famous landscaper. He demanded that only native vegetation be used and that form follow function.

Olmsted's and Jensen's fame was derived chiefly from their work on large public projects. Their precepts had little influence on home grounds until the 1930s, when Thomas Church, who designed the garden at the right, rebelled against the artificiality then fashionable. The revolution he and his followers began triumphed and it continues, but its ideology remains unfettered. The American style these men shaped has been influenced by the Japanese in the Northwest and West, by the Spanish in the Southwest: but everywhere it displays a sense of place. In the hands of such stylemakers of today as Guy Greene, Lewis Clarke and Robert Royston, who describe their designs on the following pages, the results are as different as the Appalachians and the Arizona desert. Yet each one, true to basic principles established in the gardens of Church, celebrates the natural beauty of the American countryside.

Natural beauty—a dell beyond a tea-tree—opens past the wall of a California garden by Thomas Church.

Church: adapting the beauty of nature

In Thomas Church's La Jolla garden, the natural grace of a pair of plane trees dominates the terrace, which is paved to provide space for entertaining. Church prefers native plants and trees, and though the design was deftly contrived to carry the eye from point to point, the shrubbery in the background bespeaks his love of "untrammeled nature."

The garden's primary function is to provide a place where man can recapture his affinity with the soil, if only on Saturday afternoons. It must be a green oasis where memories of his bumper-to-bumper ride from work will be erased. During past attempts to achieve such a goal by beautifying his surroundings, man has tried many things—from a complete and rigid control of all plant forms, with flowers providing a delicate pattern of embroidery, to a free and untrammeled expression of undisturbed nature. Today we take the best from these two schools of thought (once bitter enemies)—the formal and the informal, the symmetrical and the picturesque, the geometric and the natural, the classic and the romantic. We still have a strong tendency to control our surroundings, but now we want garden plants to suggest by their structure the fine melancholy we expect in nature.   THOMAS CHURCH

Elsewhere in the La Jolla garden and barely visible from the plane trees (opposite page), a pair of guava trees flanks an arch carved into a hedge of shaped and towering Eugenia trees. The hedge screens out a neighboring house so that it cannot spoil the vista; the design of this garden combines, as Church intended, "the geometric and the natural."

Clarke: a local style

From a North Carolina terrace bordered with dahlias, a brick walk wends through native pines and dogwoods to one of a series of pools that Lewis Clarke calls "rondos." He considers water a universal element in diverse landscapes.

Ecological realism is taking hold. The design for Louisiana is not the design for New Hampshire. On the East Coast a concrete patio is not put in front of the living room because it would reflect summer heat; around the San Francisco Bay region the patio would be needed for that very reason. We look for ways in which we can make people more aware of the region in which they live or work. I would like them to say, after we're gone, that nobody was here, that only God did this. I try to harmonize and contrast the varying elements that the five senses perceive so that the result seems to have existed for all time, and to achieve that I use water where appropriate. It is the only garden construction material that possesses movement, sound and great characteristics of light in reflection and color. So most of our schemes involve an eternal search to emphasize these qualities of water. LEWIS CLARKE

A tiny waterfall punctuates a rock-bordered stream that, on its course toward Clarke's rondos, flows past tall loblolly pines and pampas grass (left), azaleas (center) and liriope (right, background), all indigenous to the Piedmont region. The cypress-sided cabin serves as a woodland retreat for the owner.

Greene: the desert

Designed by Guy Greene, the Tucson, Arizona, pool and garden at left harmonize rather than merge with the desert. The pool, pictured in the light of evening, is built in a cleft between two hills, and the view beyond is unobstructed.

In the Southwest, where I work, much of the historical influence is Spanish and of course the Spanish house and garden design was influenced by the Arabs during the Moorish occupation. So the garden has been a walled-in sanctuary, shutting out the desert. But there are people who love the desert and want to be part of it, and lately, without thinking about it very much, I have been leaving out the walled enclosure. In the garden pictured here, you are in the desert as soon as you step off the porch. But the desert is a harsh place and man must modify it to survive in it. I never attempt in garden design to imitate the desert, but only to do things that to me are in harmony with the desert and that reinforce the sense of what is here. The land is sharp and jagged and the plants are sharp and jagged, and I tend to use angular forms that create sharp shadows because the countryside is that way and the light is bright and clear and brittle. GUY GREENE

The pool, shown above in daylight, has asbestos-treated concrete decks that remain cool enough for walking even in summer's heat. The rocks were placed, but the varieties of native plants were not; they just grew where they are now.

Royston: the future

There was a tremendous growth of the modern garden in the past generation, and it was directly related to the contemporary house. A new life-style emerged with that house, introducing the outdoors to the indoors. The garden was no longer tacked on; it was an integral part of the house. Today's garden is no less than that, but today we know more. There is an increasing tendency to use plant materials in simpler, more natural ways and to blend them with the strong lines of the house. They complement each other. We integrate the landscape with the house. But not everybody can have one half to three quarters of an acre to let nature flourish for him alone; there's not that much landscape to go around. It stretches our resources too thin. Perhaps three quarters of an acre will become the large estate of the future. Most people are going to be living in apartments and having gardens in common, content with small interior patios which are their own. In the San Francisco Bay area, there has been quite a tendency to town houses with common maintenance and only a little private patio, each fenced in. The gate in the fence opens into the public area, with the pool and recreation and lawn areas. It makes a lot of sense. ROBERT ROYSTON

Recalling the colonial New England village, with its homes circling a common green, The Knoll at Peacock Gap, San Rafael, California, clusters jagged rows of town houses around a shared garden that includes a swimming pool (center) and a shuffleboard court to the left of the pool. The design by Robert Royston and his associates gives each home its own tiny fenced patio (far right) in which the residents may putter if they so wish. But the common garden frees them of most maintenance responsibilities—and provides spaciousness and conveniences none could expect in a private landscape.

An encyclopedia of selected plants for landscaping 5

With thousands of species of plants available for landscaping, it is not surprising that homeowners sometimes get confused about which ones to choose, and where and how to use them. In this chapter you will find descriptions and uses of what I consider to be the best representatives of nine main groups of plant materials that can be grown in various areas of the United States and Canada. The selections are personal, and far from all-inclusive.

In each entry, the characteristics of the plant and its dimensions at maturity are based on average growing conditions and normal care. Areas for which the plants are especially recommended are designated by letters keyed to the map on page 154. If you want a ground cover to plant in a shady spot, for example, find your area letter on this map, then run through "Ground covers" beginning on page 145; where you see your area letter in the box set aside for it, read the entry to find out that ground cover's characteristics, including whether it is shade tolerant or not.

In each group, plants are listed alphabetically and described under their Latin botanical names. In these names—for example, *Prunus subhirtella pendula* (weeping Higan cherry)—the first word, in this case *Prunus,* is the name of the genus, a category of plants whose leaves, flowers and seeds bear characteristics in common. The second word—*subhirtella*—is the name of the species, of which there may be several varieties. The third word, when used, describes such a variety—in this case *pendula,* or weeping. Common genus names are cross referenced to their Latin equivalents; for example, if you want to find a description of the Norway maple and do not know its botanical name, look under "maple", where you will be referred to *Acer.*

Descriptions of deciduous trees begin on page 100; deciduous shrubs, page 113; narrow-leaved evergreen trees, page 120; broad-leaved evergreen trees, page 125; narrow-leaved evergreen shrubs, page 131; broad-leaved evergreen shrubs, page 134; ground covers, page 145; vines, page 148; and palms, page 152.

The diverse beauty of landscaping elements is shown in a potpourri: a Norway maple leaf against a white pine, and (clockwise from top left) a forsythia bush, English ivy, Douglas fir leaves and cone, a clematis blossom, the acorn of a red oak, a flowering dogwood tree, white pine needles, rhododendron leaves, a butterfly palm and viburnum berries.

AMUR MAPLE
Acer ginnala

BLOODLEAF JAPANESE MAPLE
Acer palmatum atropurpureum

NORWAY MAPLE
Acer platanoides

Deciduous trees

Deciduous trees are the dominant features in many home landscapes and if chosen with care can perform many valuable tasks. Some make excellent shade trees, their leaves keeping a house or patio cool in summer, their bare branches letting winter sunshine through. Others are especially suited to act as windbreaks or privacy screens; still others are beautiful ornaments standing on their own, graceful in shape and providing blossoms, fruit, fall colors, or all three. Some make good "street trees" because they have relatively straight trunks and high branches, require little care, and are able to grow in the compacted soil common to roadsides as well as to withstand automobile fumes and the salt used to melt icy roads.

Fast-growing deciduous trees add 2 to 3 feet a year to their height; moderate growth is about 18 inches; slow growth, about 8 to 12 inches. In the illustrations, some trees are shown while relatively young, others at a more mature age; the lower trunks of some have been omitted to show them to best advantage.

ACER (MAPLE)

The larger members of this family grow to more than 100 feet and make excellent trees for heavy shade because of their dense foliage and wide-spreading branches. Their large, overlapping leaves provide such good shade, in fact, that only the most shade-tolerant plants will grow beneath them. Most species deliver a bonus of brilliant autumn color. Red-leaved varieties of the smaller Oriental maples are grown primarily as ornamental trees and are especially suited to small suburban lots. All maples bear winglike seeds and flourish in almost any garden soil over a wide climate range. They are relatively pest and disease free.

A. circinatum (vine maple)

A small ornamental species of exceptional beauty that usually grows 12 to 15 feet high, the vine maple is similar to the better-known Japanese maple *(below)*, but takes its name from multiple trunks that assume interesting twisted shapes. It bears small drooping clusters of white and purple blossoms in early spring.   AREAS: I

A. ginnala (Amur maple)

This small (to 20 feet) tree or shrub has fragrant, greenish yellow flowers in spring, red fruit in summer and scarlet leaves in fall.   AREAS: A B C F H I

A. palmatum varieties (Japanese maple)

The most popular Japanese maples are selected for their delicate form and lacy, star-shaped red leaves, although there are green-leaved varieties. They are relatively slow growing and seldom reach 20 feet. One of the hardiest and best varieties, the bloodleaf Japanese maple *(A. palmatum atropurpureum)*, bears dark red leaves throughout the summer.   AREAS: C D I J

A. platanoides and varieties (Norway maple)

A good shade and street tree, the Norway maple grows rapidly to a height of 70 to 90 feet and has small yellow flowers in spring; the large green leaves turn bright yellow in fall. Two varieties, the Crimson King Norway maple and Fassen's Black Norway maple, have purplish red leaves through the summer. Norway maples have extensive surface roots that add to the difficulty of growing anything in their dense shade.   AREAS: B C D F I J

A. rubrum (red maple, scarlet maple, swamp maple)
This fast-growing species reaches 70 to 90 feet, thrives in moist to marshy soil and provides both shade and color; its small red flowers appear very early in spring and are soon followed by bright red fruit. Its leaves are among the first to turn color in fall—red, yellow, orange or combinations of all three.   AREAS: B C D E ☐ ☐ I J

A. saccharum (sugar maple, rock maple)
The sugar maple, source of maple syrup, is a fast-growing, sturdy shade tree that reaches heights of 70 to 100 feet. Its leaves (Canada's national symbol) turn yellow, orange and sometimes scarlet in fall.   AREAS: A B C ☐ F ☐ H I

AESCULUS (HORSE CHESTNUT)

A. carnea briotti (ruby horse chestnut)
Large handsome trees with well-rounded crowns set on sturdy trunks, ruby horse chestnuts ultimately grow to 75 feet in rich, moist soil, but are commonly only 30 to 40 feet tall. They produce bright pink-to-red flowers in 10-inch upright clusters for two weeks in midspring. They are relatively messy trees, with a habit of dropping their leaves and inedible fruit.   AREAS: A B C ☐ F ☐ I J

ALBIZIA

A. julibrissin and varieties (silk tree)
A spreading ornamental tree with graceful, almost fernlike leaves, the silk tree grows to 35 feet, often on multiple trunks, and produces fluffy pink blossoms from midsummer to early fall. A smaller variety, *A. julibrissin rosea,* is especially hardy.   AREAS: ☐ C D E ☐ G ☐ I J

AMELANCHIER (SERVICEBERRY, SHAD-BLOW)

Members of this genus are decorative during much of the year. Their small white flowers are borne in great profusion in early spring, before the leaves. In early summer, small edible red or black berries appear and are quickly eaten by birds. The fall foliage is yellow or red.

A. canadensis (shad-blow or downy serviceberry)
This species eventually becomes 40 to 60 feet tall and has an upright, often narrow, habit of growth. Its foliage is especially attractive in early spring, when the new leaves are a soft grayish color.   AREAS: ☐ B C D ☐ G H I

A. grandiflora (apple serviceberry)
The apple serviceberry grows 20 to 25 feet tall with wide-spreading branches and dense foliage. Its white flowers resemble apple blossoms.   AREAS: ☐ B C D ☐ G H I

ASH See *Fraxinus*
ASH, MOUNTAIN See *Sorbus*
BASSWOOD See *Tilia*

BAUHINIA

B. variegata (Buddhist bauhinia, mountain ebony, orchid tree)
This umbrella-shaped ornamental tree grows 20 or 25 feet tall and presents a dazzling display of orchidlike flowers, 2 to 3 inches across and lavender to purple in color, in late winter and early spring. The light green leaves usually fall in midwinter.   AREAS: ☐ ☐ E ☐ ☐ ☐ J

BEECH See *Fagus*

BETULA (BIRCH)

Birches are grown, singly or in groups, for their handsome white bark (not all have it), their graceful stance, their

RED MAPLE, SCARLET MAPLE, SWAMP MAPLE
Acer rubrum

SUGAR MAPLE, ROCK MAPLE
Acer saccharum

HARDY SILK TREE
Albizia julibrissin rosea

Key letters refer to growing areas shown on map, page 154.   101

CUTLEAF EUROPEAN BIRCH
Betula pendula gracilis

KATSURA TREE
Cercidiphyllum japonicum

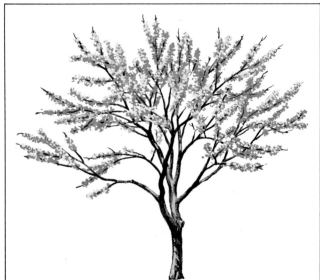

EASTERN REDBUD
Cercis canadensis

light, dappled shade and the yellow of their leaves in fall. Most do well in wet soil, and some, such as the species listed below, will grow in dry, gravelly soil where other trees fail. As a group birches are subject to attack by insects such as birch-leaf miners and bronze birch borers, and ordinarily need to be sprayed to maintain their beauty.

B. paprifera (canoe birch, paper birch, white birch)
The canoe birch can grow to 90 feet, although it usually reaches only half that height in gardens. It is less prone to disease than other white-barked birches and has fewer black markings. AREAS: A B   F   H I

B. pendula and varieties (European white birch)
The many varieties of this birch, which may grow from 30 to 60 feet tall, permit a wide selection of tree shapes—from the slender, gracefully pendulous branches of the *gracilis* to the columnar *fastigiata*. AREAS: A B C D   F   H I J

BIRCH See *Betula*
BLACK GUM See *Nyssa*

CASTANEA (CHESTNUT)
C. mollissima (Chinese chestnut)
Apparently resistant to the fungus disease that has all but eliminated the native American species, the Chinese chestnut makes a pleasing shade tree of good size (30 to 50 feet), often with several branching trunks and long lustrous leaves that turn yellow to bronze in autumn. Grown in groups of two or more, Chinese chestnuts cross-pollinate to produce edible nuts. AREAS: C D   G   I

CELTIS (HACKBERRY)
C. laevigata reticulata, also called *C. douglasii*
(netleaf hackberry, western hackberry)
An ornamental tree that grows 25 to 30 feet tall with a similar spread, the netleaf hackberry is a good shade tree that tolerates many conditions, including the polluted air of cities. In summer and fall it bears small, sweet-tasting black berries among elmlike leaves. AREAS: C D   G

CERCIDIPHYLLUM
C. japonicum (katsura tree)
This wide-spreading shade tree grows to 60 to 100 feet; its open foliage allows for ample air circulation beneath, and its graceful, heart-shaped leaves turn yellow to scarlet in fall. The trees are columnar when young but may develop several trunks. AREAS: B C D E   G   I J

CERCIS (REDBUD)
C. canadensis (eastern redbud)
C. reniformis (Texas redbud)
The redbud has leaves like the katsura's *(above)* but grows only 25 to 35 feet tall. Pink-to-white flowers bloom in spring. *C. canadensis* AREAS: B C D E   G   I J
C. reinformis AREAS: G

CHERRY See *Prunus*
CHESTNUT See *Castanea*
CHESTNUT, HORSE See *Aesculus*
CHINESE FLAME TREE See *Koelreuteria*

CHIONANTHUS
C. virginicus (fringe tree)
This ornamental, shrublike tree, which grows to 25 or 30 feet, bears 5- to 8-inch feathery clusters of white flowers in late spring or early summer, just after the leaves, which appear later than those of most other plants. Blue, grapelike

fruit follows the flowers on female trees; the leaves turn yellow in fall.　　　AREAS: B C D E G I J

CLADRASTIS (YELLOWWOOD)
C. lutea (American yellowwood)
A handsome, full-bodied, exceedingly drought-resistant tree that grows 30 to 50 feet tall, the yellowwood bears pendulous clusters of white-to-pink fragrant flowers in early summer, but may not flower every year. Its leaves turn yellow and orange in fall.　　　AREAS: B C D E G I J

CORK TREE See *Phellodendron*

CORNUS (DOGWOOD)
Trees for all seasons, dogwoods rank at or near the top of most lists of ornamentals wherever they can be grown. Their horizontal branches with gently up-curved ends display showers of spring blooms, white in most species but pink in some. In summer they provide fine, open shade and bear clusters of red fruit; in fall the leaves turn a deep red. Dogwoods flower best in sun but tolerate light shade. *(See also Deciduous shrubs, page 114.)*

C. florida and varieties (flowering dogwood)
Familiar in the woods and along highways from southern New England to Florida and Texas, the flowering dogwood grows 20 to 40 feet tall and is a most desirable species for lawn and patio use. Pink-flowering varieties are attractive planted alone or in combination with the more common white-flowered ones.　　　AREAS: C D E G I J

C. kousa (Japanese dogwood)
Where space is at a premium, the smaller (15 to 20 feet), profusely blooming Japanese dogwood should be considered. It blooms about three weeks after native species and bears flowers for almost a month. Its pinkish red fruits resemble raspberries.　　　AREAS: C D E G I J

C. nuttallii (Pacific dogwood)
This species' 4- to 5-inch blossoms sometimes appear in fall as well as in spring along the West Coast, where it is native. Wild trees may grow 75 feet tall, but most garden trees mature at 30 to 40 feet.　　　AREAS:　　　　　 I J

COTTONWOOD See *Populus*
CRAB APPLE See *Malus*
CRAPE MYRTLE See *Lagerstroemia*

CRATAEGUS (HAWTHORN)
Hawthorns are small, often shrublike trees used for display and for hedges. Most species are dense, twiggy and thorny and bear showy white flowers and red, orange or yellow fruit that hangs on after the leaves have fallen.

C. mollis (downy hawthorn)
The downy hawthorn, named for its fuzzy leaves, reaches heights of 20 to 30 feet. It bears small, red, pear-shaped fruit in fall.　　　AREAS: B C D F G H I

C. mordenensis 'Toba' (Toba hawthorn)
This hardy hybrid has glossy foliage and fragrant pink flowers that turn a deep rose as they mature. They are followed by bright red berries.　　　AREAS: A B C D F G H I

C. oxyacantha and varieties (English hawthorn)
The English hawthorn, which grows about 15 feet tall, includes colorful varieties such as *C. oxyacantha pauli,* which has showy scarlet double flowers; *C. oxyacantha plena,*

PINK FLOWERING DOGWOOD
Cornus florida rubra

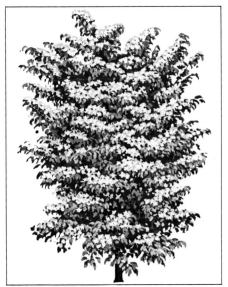

JAPANESE DOGWOOD
Cornus kousa

PACIFIC DOGWOOD
Cornus nuttallii

Key letters refer to growing areas shown on map, page 154.　　　103

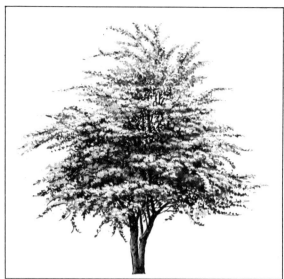

WASHINGTON HAWTHORN
Crataegus phaenopyrum

RIVERS PURPLE BEECH
Fagus sylvatica riversii

MARSHALL'S SEEDLESS ASH
Fraxinus pennsylvanica lanceolata 'Marshall's Seedless'

which produces double white flowers; and *C. oxyacantha rosea-plena,* which bears pale pink double blossoms in clusters.　　　　AREAS: B C D ⬚ ⬚ ⬚ I ⬚

C. phaenopyrum (Washington hawthorn)
The handsomest of hawthorns, this species grows 25 to 30 feet high and bears white blossoms late in spring, followed by small, bright red berries. Its leaves turn scarlet to orange in fall.　　　AREAS: B C D ⬚ F G H I ⬚

DELONIX (POINCIANA)
D. regia (poinciana regia, royal poinciana, flame tree)
The poinciana, among the showiest of the tropical trees, has fernlike foliage and huge clusters of dazzling scarlet and yellow flowers in summer. It grows rapidly to 25 to 40 feet in a wide-branching shape.　AREAS: ⬚ ⬚ ⬚ E ⬚ ⬚ J

DOGWOOD See *Cornus*

ELAEAGNUS
(See also Deciduous shrubs, page 115, and Broad-leaved evergreen shrubs, page 137.)
E. angustifolia (Russian olive, oleaster)
A good choice for shade, windbreaks or screens, the Russian olive has a wide-spreading bushlike form and attractive gray-green leaves that are silvery on the undersides. It is hardy and drought resistant and will grow in almost any soil to a height of 20 to 30 feet. Its tiny yellow flowers, inconspicuous but intensely fragrant, are followed by yellowish berries.　AREAS: A B C ⬚ ⬚ F G H I ⬚

ELM See *Ulmus*
EMPRESS TREE See *Paulownia*

FAGUS (BEECH)
F. sylvatica and varieties (European beech)
These handsome trees grow 70 to 90 feet tall in oval to broadly pyramidal shapes with sturdy trunks, smooth gray bark and shiny leaves that range from green in *F. sylvatica* to red-to-purple in *F. sylvatica riversii* to deep bronze in the copper beech. Since their shallow root systems add to the difficulty of growing grass or other plants in their heavy shade, they are often left unpruned so that their foliage almost touches the ground.　AREAS: B C D ⬚ ⬚ ⬚ I ⬚

FLAME TREE See *Delonix*
FLAME TREE, CHINESE See *Koelreuteria*

FRAXINUS (ASH)
Vigorous, fast-growing trees that provide high, medium-to-light shade, ashes have tall, stately trunks. The leaves of most species turn yellow to deep purple in fall. *(See also Broad-leaved evergreen trees, page 128.)*

F. pennsylvanica lanceolata 'Marshall's seedless'
(Marshall's seedless ash)
One of the most popular ashes, this species does not reproduce itself in the form of unwanted seedlings, a major problem with most ashes. It has fine, glossy leaves and a pyramidal growth habit while young. Tolerant of all soils, it grows 50 to 60 feet tall.　AREAS: A B C D E F G H I J

F. velutina glabra (Modesto ash)
The Modesto ash does well in dry, alkaline soils and is a popular street and shade tree in the Southwest, where it grows 40 to 50 feet tall.　AREAS: ⬚ ⬚ ⬚ ⬚ ⬚ G ⬚ I J

FRINGE TREE See *Chionanthus*

GINKGO
G. biloba (ginkgo, maidenhair tree)
Handsome street or shade trees with delicate, fan-shaped leaves that turn yellow in fall, ginkgos are ungainly when young, but become wide spreading and fan shaped as they grow slowly to heights of 70 to 100 feet. Mature female trees bear foul-smelling fruit. AREAS: B C D | F G | I J

GLEDITSIA (HONEY LOCUST)
G. triacanthos inermis and varieties
(thornless honey locust)
Honey locusts tolerate exhaust fumes and soot, and the thornless variety is a popular street or light-shade tree for cities and inner suburbs. It grows 70 to 100 feet tall in a graceful, fountainlike shape with fernlike foliage. Varieties such as *G. triacanthos inermis* 'Moraine' also lack the messy podlike fruit of the species. AREAS: B C D | F G | I J

GUM, BLACK See *Nyssa*
GUM, SOUR See *Nyssa*
GUM, SWEET See *Liquidambar*
HACKBERRY See *Celtis*

HALESIA (SILVERBELL)
H. carolina (Carolina silverbell)
A small ornamental tree, growing 15 to 30 feet tall, the silverbell bears a profusion of small, white, bell-shaped flowers in early spring. The leaves turn soft shades of yellow in fall. AREAS: C D E | I

HAWTHORN See *Crataegus*
HONEY LOCUST See *Gleditsia*
HORSE CHESTNUT See *Aesculus*

JACARANDA
J. acutifolia (sharpleaf jacaranda)
Clusters of 2-inch-long lavender-blue flowers in summer and fall and fernlike foliage on spreading branches make this tree a favorite, whether it is used as a screen or a street tree or planted purely for its beauty. It grows rapidly to 35 to 50 feet tall. AREAS: E | J

KATSURA TREE See *Cercidiphyllum*

KOELREUTERIA
K. formosana (Chinese flame tree)
K. paniculata (golden-rain tree, varnish tree)
Both species bear large drooping clusters of small yellow flowers in early summer and bladderlike seed pods in late summer and fall. The flame tree's pods are red and orange; the golden-rain tree produces less showy yellow-to-brown pods. Both grow rapidly to 20 to 40 feet and do best in full sun.
　　　K. formosana AREAS: E | J
　　　K. paniculata AREAS: C D E | G | I J

LABURNUM
L. watereri, also called *L. vossii* (Waterer laburnum)
Reaching 20 to 30 feet in height, with green bark, cloverlike leaves and stiffly upright branches, this species produces pendulous clusters of pealike yellow blossoms in late spring or early summer. AREAS: C D | G | I

LAGERSTROEMIA
L. indica and varieties (crape myrtle)
These small ornamental trees, which grow to 20 feet, are notable for their white, pink, red, lavender or bluish flowers, which have a crinkled, crapelike texture. Blooms appear in midsummer. AREAS: D E | G | J

MODESTO ASH
Fraxinus velutina glabra

MORAINE THORNLESS HONEY LOCUST
Gleditsia triacanthos inermis 'Moraine'

CRAPE MYRTLE
Lagerstroemia indica

Key letters refer to growing areas shown on map, page 154.

SWEET GUM
Liquidambar styraciflua

SAUCER MAGNOLIA
Magnolia soulangeana

LILAC See *Syringa*
LINDEN See *Tilia*

LIQUIDAMBAR

L. styraciflua (sweet gum)

A handsome, pyramidal shade tree that grows 60 to 80 feet tall, the sweet gum is particularly noted for its glossy disease- and pest-resistant foliage, which is dark green in summer, turning shades of yellow to deep crimson in fall. Its fruits are horned balls that fall after the leaves drop, creating a minor cleanup problem.   AREAS: C D E   I J

LIRIODENDRON

L. tulipifera (tulip tree)

Fast growing and broadly pyramidal, this tree easily reaches heights over 100 feet with a spread of 40 feet or more, making it an excellent choice as a large shade tree. Its dense, dark green, pest-resistant leaves are tuliplike in outline and turn yellow in fall. Greenish yellow, tulip-shaped flowers, touched with deep orange at the base of each petal, appear in late spring.   AREAS: B C D E   I J

LOCUST, HONEY See *Gleditsia*

MAGNOLIA

Magnolias are among the first trees to burst into blossom in the spring—with spectacular, generally fragrant flowers that range up to 10 inches in diameter and from white to pink to reddish purple in color. The foliage that follows is dark green, luxuriant and pest resistant, and the smooth, gray bark is decorative throughout the year. Despite their lovely appearance, magnolias are tough enough to tolerate city conditions. *(See also Broad-leaved evergreen trees, page 128.)*

M. denudata (Yulan magnolia)

Moderately fast growing, with a broad, rounded outline, this tree reaches 30 to 40 feet and bears 6-inch fragrant white blossoms in midspring.   AREAS: C D E G I J

M. loebneri 'Merrill' (Merrill magnolia)

Fast growing and pyramidal in shape, the Merrill magnolia reaches 25 to 50 feet and bears fragrant white flowers in early spring.   AREAS: C D E G I J

M. soulangeana and varieties (saucer magnolia)

Among the most popular magnolias, these trees grow 20 to 25 feet tall and produce 5- to 10-inch cup-shaped blossoms; the colors range from white to pink to deep rose purple, depending on the variety.   AREAS: C D E G I J

M. stellata (star magnolia)

This slow-growing spreading species bears its fragrant, white double flowers, which are 3 to 4 inches across, so early they are sometimes nipped by frost, particularly in protected spots where the trees flower at the first hint of warm weather. The star magnolia, whose lower branches may trail to the ground, resembles a large shrub but may reach a height of 20 feet.   AREAS: C D E G I J

M. virginiana, also called M. glauca (sweet bay)

Tall and evergreen in southern climates, the sweet bay in cooler regions is a small, globular, deciduous tree or large shrub seldom exceeding 20 feet in height. The 3-inch flowers, white, waxy and very fragrant, appear from late spring through early summer among deep green leaves that have whitish undersides. The species can be grown in very wet as well as average soil.   AREAS: C

MAIDENHAIR TREE See *Ginkgo*

MALUS (CRAB APPLE)
Crab apples, which come in many species and varieties, are among the fastest growing and most beautiful of the flowering trees, bearing a profusion of lovely white, pink or red blossoms in early spring. The red or yellow fruits that follow, ranging from less than ¼ inch to over 2 inches in diameter, are decorative, attract birds, and can be made into a tasty jelly. Foliage is generally dense and dark green. Most flowering crab apples grow 15 to 25 feet tall (although there are varieties that grow to only 8 feet) in shapes varying from narrow and upright to broad, rounded or pendulous. They are highly popular as single trees or in small groups. One extremely hardy species, *M. baccata* (Siberian crab apple), grows well in Areas A and H, to a height of 50 feet. Many flowering crab apples bear light and heavy crops of flowers and fruit in alternate years; *M.* 'Dorothea' is a variety that can be depended upon every year to have a massive display of semidouble flowers and small, bright yellow fruit.   AREAS: A B C D   F G H I

MAPLE See *Acer*

MORUS (MULBERRY)
M. alba 'Kingan' (fruitless mulberry, Kingan mulberry)
A fast-growing drought-resistant species that reaches 30 to 40 feet in height, this tree has spreading branches and foliage that provides dense shade, without the nuisance of messy berries that makes most mulberries objectionable for garden use.   AREAS: B C D E F G H I J

MOUNTAIN ASH See *Sorbus*
MOUNTAIN EBONY See *Bauhinia*
MULBERRY See *Morus*
MYRTLE, CRAPE See *Lagerstroemia*

NYSSA
N. sylvatica (black tupelo, black gum, sour gum, pepperidge)
The black tupelo is pyramidal, with distinctive horizontal branches, and is one of the best lawn trees for fall color; its deep green, glossy leaves become brilliant scarlet to orange in early fall. In late summer female trees bear clusters of grapelike blue berries relished by birds. Slow growing, the trees reach heights of 30 to 70 feet and do best in moist, acid soil.   AREAS: B C D E   I

OAK See *Quercus*
OLEASTER See *Elaeagnus*
OLIVE, RUSSIAN See *Elaeagnus*
ORCHID TREE See *Bauhinia*

OXYDENDRUM
O. arboreum (sorrel tree, sourwood)
This graceful slow-growing tree, which rarely exceeds 25 feet in height, has bronze-tinted leaves that turn a lustrous green in summer, when pendant clusters of white bell-shaped blossoms appear; in late summer the foliage becomes bright scarlet. The dry seed pods stay on the tree through much of the winter.   AREAS: C D   I

PAGODA TREE See *Sophora*

PARKINSONIA (THORN)
P. aculeata (Jerusalem thorn)
An open-branching tree with sparse foliage and fragrant yellow flowers in spring, the Jerusalem thorn grows to

DOROTHEA CRAB APPLE
Malus 'Dorothea'

SORREL TREE, SOURWOOD
Oxydendrum arboreum

Key letters refer to growing areas shown on map, page 154.   107

15 to 30 feet. Since its twigs have inch-long spines, it can be clipped to form a hedge. It tolerates drought and does well in light, sandy soil.　　　AREAS:▯▯▯E▯▯·J

PAULOWNIA
P. tomentosa (empress tree, royal paulownia)
This fast-growing, rounded tree grows to 35 or 40 feet in almost any soil and bears masses of 2-inch-long, fragrant violet flowers in spring. Its extremely large coarse-textured leaves, which appear later and may be 2 to 3 feet across, provide dense shade. The trees tolerate both city and seaside conditions.　　　AREAS:▯▯C D E▯G▯I J

PEAR See *Pyrus*
PEPPERIDGE See *Nyssa*

PHELLODENDRON (CORK TREE)
P. amurense (Amur cork tree)
Fast growing to 30 feet, often with a greater spread, the Amur cork tree is a good choice for light shade. Its loose, open leaves appear late in spring and turn yellow and drop early in fall, when female trees bear small black berries. Huge branches and fissured, corklike bark make the tree decorative through winter.　　　AREAS:A B C D▯F G H I▯

PISTACIA
P. chinensis (Chinese pistache)
A broad, rounded tree that grows slowly to 40 to 50 feet, the Chinese pistache makes a handsome ornamental planting. Its fine-textured, dark green foliage casts good shade and turns bright red and orange in fall; it withstands heat and drought, thrives in most soils and is free of disease and pests. Female trees bear dense clusters of small, bright red nuts in fall.　　　AREAS:▯▯▯E▯▯▯J

PLANE TREE See *Platanus*

PLATANUS (PLANE TREE, SYCAMORE)
These handsome wide-spreading and fast-growing trees are popular as shade and street trees. The leaves are large and coarse-textured, and the brown, ball-like seed clusters that appear in fall hang from the branches through the winter. The bark is distinctive; the older bark peels in irregular patches to disclose the smooth, lighter inner bark. All species are tolerant of most soils but are subject to sycamore blight, which kills twigs and young branches unless controlled with fungicide sprays.

P. acerifolia (London plane tree)
The London plane, often used as a street tree, has a straight trunk and grows in a rounded shape up to 100 feet tall. It is one of the species most resistant to twig blight and withstands city pollution.　　　AREAS:▯▯C D E F G▯I J

P. racemosa (California plane tree)
An especially picturesque tree that can grow to 120 feet, this species often has several trunks, and its branches grow in irregular, twisted patterns.　　　AREAS:▯▯▯▯▯▯▯▯J

PLUM See *Prunus*
POINCIANA See *Delonix*

POPULUS (POPLAR, COTTONWOOD)
P. alba pyramidalis, also known as *P. bolleana*
(Bolleana poplar)
This narrow, columnar tree grows 70 to 90 feet tall; its gray-green leaves, which show their whitish undersides when ruffled by a breeze, turn red in fall. The Bolleana pop-

CHINESE PISTACHE
Pistacia chinensis

lar, like other poplars, is very fast growing, but has weak branches that break in windstorms or when ice laden. Since its wide-spreading roots seek out moisture and can disrupt drainage fields and sewage pipes, it should be planted well away from them.　　　　　AREAS:|A|B|C|D|　|F|G|H|I|J|

PRUNUS (PLUM, CHERRY)

The members of this genus that are prized for their blossoms rather than their fruit are among the most beautiful of ornamental trees. Those listed are low growing (to 40 feet) and thus well suited to small properties. To bloom their best, they should have full sun and a normally moist soil. *(See also Deciduous shrubs, page 117, and Broadleaved evergreen shrubs, page 143.)*

P. blireiana (Blireiana plum, purpleleaf plum)
Small pink double flowers appear in early spring before the dark purplish red leaves, which are borne on slender, graceful branches. The trees grow 18 to 20 feet tall and bear small, purplish red fruit.　　AREAS:|　|B|C|D|E|F|G|　|I|J|

P. cerasifera 'Thundercloud' (Thundercloud plum)
Similar to *P. blireiana* in shape and foliage and blossom color, this plum sometimes produces a crop of small but edible red fruit.　　　　　AREAS:|　|B|C|D|E|F|G|H|I|J|

P. serrulata varieties (Oriental cherry)
Some 50 varieties of this outstanding species are grown in North America. They bear pink or white, single or double flowers, ½ to 2 inches across, fragrant in some varieties; blossoms open before or with the leaves. One of the hardiest and most popular varieties is *P. serrulata* 'Kwanzan' (Kwanzan cherry), which bears large, deep pink double blossoms and reddish foliage.　　AREAS:|　|　|C|D|　|　|　|　|I|J|

P. subhirtella varieties (Higan cherry)
These trees bloom in early spring before the leaves appear; *P. subhirtella autumnalis* may send forth its small semidouble pink blossoms during a mild autumn as well. *P. subhirtella pendula* (weeping Higan cherry) is an especially lovely tree, with cascading branches that often hang down to the ground and bear a profusion of small single pink blossoms.　　　　AREAS:|　|　|C|D|　|　|　|　|I|J|

P. yedoensis (Yoshino cherry)
The bushy Yoshino cherry is one of the species that delights visitors to the Tidal Basin in Washington, D.C., each April. Its small, slightly fragrant single blossoms range from very pale blush pink to nearly white and open before the leaves appear.　　　　　　AREAS:|　|　|C|D|　|　|　|　|I|J|

PYRUS (PEAR)
(See also Broad-leaved evergreen trees, page 130.)
P. calleryana 'Bradford' (Bradford callery pear)
Narrowly pyramidal with upswept branches, this species grows 30 to 50 feet tall and makes a good street or ornamental tree. It has shiny, leathery, dark green leaves that turn deep red to scarlet in fall and lovely small white blossoms in spring. The russet-colored fruit is tiny and inconspicuous. The Bradford variety is less susceptible to fire blight than most pears.　　AREAS:|　|B|C|D|　|G|　|I|J|

QUERCUS (OAK)

Most oaks grow more than 50 feet tall and often as wide and make fine street or shade trees on larger lots. They are hardy, dependable trees that grow well in most soils, with branches strong enough to resist damage from wind, ice or snow. Many have large, handsome, deeply

LONDON PLANE TREE
Platanus acerifolia

KWANZAN CHERRY
Prunus serrulata 'Kwanzan'

Key letters refer to growing areas shown on map, page 154.　　　　　　109

lobed leaves and are noted for their fall color. *(See also Broad-leaved evergreen trees, page 130.)*

Q. alba (white oak)
This oak is broad and spreading with widely spaced, massive, horizontal branches. The leaves turn purplish red in fall and often remain during winter. The trees grow slowly but can reach 150 feet tall; their long taproots make them hard to transplant. AREAS: B C D F G H I

Q. borealis (northern red oak)
A superior shade tree, the northern red oak transplants easily, grows faster than most oaks, to 60 to 75 feet, and tolerates city conditions. AREAS: A B C D F G H I J

Q. coccinea (scarlet oak)
Named for its bright fall color, this tree has more open foliage than most oaks. Trees grow 60 to 75 feet tall and are difficult to transplant. AREAS: B C D F G H I

Q. nigra (water oak)
The water oak, which tolerates wet soils, is conical or round topped, with slender wide-spreading branches and small, wedge-shaped bluish green leaves that cling to the trees until late fall. It reaches 60 to 75 feet and is often planted as a street tree. AREAS: D E

Q. palustris (pin oak)
The pin oak is notable for the symmetrical, pyramidal growth of its many branches, which point almost straight up at the top, straight out at the middle and downward toward the bottom. The leaves turn scarlet in fall. Easy to transplant, the tree does well in all but alkaline soils and grows 60 to 75 feet tall. AREAS: B C D E F I J

Q. phellos (willow oak)
This dense-branching tree resembles the pin oak but presents a more rounded outline; it is notable for its slender, shiny, willowlike leaves, which turn yellow in autumn. It is easily transplanted and is widely used as a street or ornamental tree. AREAS: C D E F I J

RAIN TREE See *Koelreuteria*
REDBUD See *Cercis*
ROWAN TREE See *Sorbus*
RUSSIAN OLIVE See *Elaeagnus*

SALIX (WILLOW)
Weeping willows, with their graceful branches and slender leaves, rank among the loveliest and fastest-growing ornamental trees. But their wood is weak and easily cracked by wind, snow or ice; their roots can clog drainage fields, and dead twigs and branches cause litter.

S. alba tristis (golden weeping willow)
The hardiest weeping willow, this tree grows 50 to 75 feet tall. Its dark green leaves turn yellow in fall and its young branches are yellow. AREAS: A B C D F G H I J

S. babylonica (Babylon weeping willow)
The most "weeping" of all the willows, this tree, which grows to 25 feet, has dark green leaves that are grayish green on their undersides. AREAS: C D G I J

SAPIUM (TALLOW TREE)
S. sebiferum (Chinese tallow tree)
Fast growing and spreading, with picturesque branches and dense foliage, the Chinese tallow tree grows 35 to

NORTHERN RED OAK
Quercus borealis

40 feet tall; its heart-shaped, light green leaves, which flutter attractively in the breeze, turn yellow to flaming red in fall. It grows in most soils and is unusually free of disease and pests.   AREAS: □□□ E □□□ J

SCHOLAR TREE See *Sophora*
SERVICEBERRY See *Amelanchier*
SHAD-BLOW See *Amelanchier*
SILK TREE See *Albizia*
SILVERBELL See *Halesia*

SOPHORA (PAGODA TREE)
S. japonica (Japanese pagoda tree, Chinese scholar tree)
This ornamental, rounded, wide-branching species grows 50 to 75 feet tall, makes a good shade or street tree and tolerates city conditions. It blooms in late summer, with clusters of yellowish white, pealike flowers against lacy, dark green foliage. Yellowish seed pods follow and often linger through winter.   AREAS: □ BCD □ G □ I J

SORBUS (MOUNTAIN ASH, ROWAN TREE)
Fast-growing ornamental trees of small to medium size, mountain ashes have finely divided foliage and are especially colorful in spring and fall.

S. aucuparia (European mountain ash, rowan tree)
This handsome tree, slender when young, spreading with age, grows 30 to 40 feet tall and is the most popular mountain ash because of its conspicuous white blossoms, which appear late in spring, its clusters of small red berries and its open foliage.   AREAS: A B C □ F H I

S. decora (showy mountain ash)
A shrubby tree 20 to 30 feet tall, this species bears white flowers in late spring and clusters of bright red berries in early fall.   AREAS: A B C □ F H I

SORREL TREE See *Oxydendrum*
SOUR GUM See *Nyssa*
SOURWOOD See *Oxydendrum*

STEWARTIA
S. pseudocamellia (Japanese stewartia)
A spreading ornamental tree that grows 40 to 60 feet tall, the Japanese stewartia has year-round appeal. In midsummer, when few other woody plants are in bloom, it bears large, white, cup-shaped, camellialike flowers; its bright green foliage becomes purplish or bronze in fall; winter interest is created by its decorative reddish bark, which peels off in large flakes.   AREAS: □ CD □□ I J

SWEET BAY See *Magnolia*
SWEET GUM See *Liquidambar*
SYCAMORE See *Platanus*

SYRINGA (LILAC)
(See also Deciduous shrubs, page 119.)
S. amurensis japonica (Japanese tree lilac)
Creamy white flower spikes—sometimes 6 inches long —appear in late spring and make this pyramidal, 30-foot tree decorative weeks after other lilacs have faded. Since their blossoms have an unpleasant odor, the tree lilac should be planted where its beauty can be admired from a slight distance. Shiny cherrylike bark lends interest after the foliage has fallen.   AREAS: A B C D □ F H I

TALLOW TREE See *Sapium*
THORN See *Parkinsonia*

GOLDEN WEEPING WILLOW
Salix alba tristis

EUROPEAN MOUNTAIN ASH, ROWAN TREE
Sorbus aucuparia

Key letters refer to growing areas shown on map, page 154.

TILIA (LINDEN, BASSWOOD)

Lindens, which usually grow 60 to 90 feet tall in a pyramidal shape, are among the finest shade and street trees. Their dark green, heart-shaped leaves appear early in spring, forming a dense canopy, and cling to the branches until late fall, when they usually turn yellow. Small yellowish white flowers, inconspicuous but fragrant, appear in early summer, followed by round nutlike fruit. Lindens do best in moist soil.

T. americana (American linden)

The American linden has a compact, symmetrical shape and grows rapidly to 90 feet; it has strong wood, large coarse leaves and a straight trunk with dark gray, furrowed bark at maturity. AREAS: A B C D F H I J

T. cordata (little leaf linden)

Perhaps the finest linden, this slow-growing species reaches 50 to 70 feet and bears small dainty leaves in dense abundance. It is among the hardiest of lindens and does well in cities. AREAS: A B C D F H I J

T. tomentosa (silver linden)

Densely foliaged, with an outline so symmetrical that the tree appears to have been clipped, the silver linden is noted chiefly for its dark green leaves with silvery undersides, which give a shimmering effect in a breeze. Trees grow 50 to 70 feet tall. AREAS: B C D I J

TULIP TREE See *Liriodendron*
TUPELO See *Nyssa*

ULMUS (ELM)

Unlike the American elm, which is plagued by Dutch elm disease, the species listed below—while not so majestic or tall growing—are disease resistant. And because they are smaller than the American elm they are better suited for landscape use on small properties. They are easily transplanted and grow vigorously in most soils. *(See also Broad-leaved evergreen trees, page 131.)*

U. parvifolia (Chinese elm)

A fast-growing round-topped tree, the Chinese elm grows to heights of 40 to 50 feet and has dark green serrated leaves. Unlike most other elms, whose leaves turn yellow in fall, the Chinese species has foliage that turns red or purple and clings to the branches after most other trees have shed their leaves. Its flaking bark provides a decorative, mottled effect. AREAS: C D E G I J

U. pumila 'Coolshade' (Coolshade Siberian elm)

This round-headed elm, which grows 50 to 75 feet tall, thrives in most climates and poor soil; its wood, stronger than the Siberian elm's *(U. pumila)*, resists breakage from wind, snow and ice. AREAS: C D E F G H I J

VARNISH TREE See *Koelreuteria*
WILLOW See *Salix*
YELLOWWOOD See *Cladrastis*

ZELKOVA

Z. serrata (Japanese zelkova)

Related to the elm, but resistant to Dutch elm disease, this tree is elmlike in its rounded shape, wide-spreading branches and serrated leaves, and is a good choice for a large shade tree. It grows rapidly when young and reaches heights of 70 to 90 feet. The leaves turn yellow to russet in fall. AREAS: C D G I J

LITTLE LEAF LINDEN
Tilia cordata

Deciduous shrubs

The brightest spots in many gardens are those occupied by deciduous shrubs, which come in virtually every size and shape, from low, rounded types with modest flowers to tall, arching specimens that resemble fountain sprays. While some have notable fall color, the main asset of most is their spectacular spring and summer show of blossoms and, in many cases, fruit. Many shrubs provide year-round interest. As early as February in warmer regions, the buds of some species begin to sprout and the parade of color goes on until late October; the berries of a few varieties, distasteful to birds, stay on through the winter. Most species, except for moderate pruning, require little care, and most reach mature size rapidly, often within five years. Fast-growing types may make 3 or more feet of growth a year if tips are not pruned to encourage side growth; moderate-growing species add about 2 feet a year and slow-growing ones about a foot.

ALMOND See *Prunus*
AZALEA See *Rhododendron*
BARBERRY See *Berberis*
BEAUTY BUSH See *Kolkwitzia*

BERBERIS (BARBERRY)
(See also Broad-leaved evergreen shrubs, page 134.)
B. thunbergii and varieties (Japanese barberry)
The upright fast-growing Japanese barberries have thorny, closely spaced branches that make them ideal barrier hedges. The shrubs grow 4 to 7 feet tall and have tiny yellow blossoms in spring and bright red foliage in fall. Small, mealy, red berries appear in late summer and remain through the winter.   AREAS: B C D F G H I J

BLUEBEARD See *Caryopteris*
BRIDALWREATH See *Spiraea*
BROOM See *Cytisus*

BUDDLEIA
B. davidii (orange-eyed butterfly bush)
This fast-growing, loosely spreading shrub has gray-green foliage and grows up to 20 feet tall in frost-free climates. Its lilac-like purple blossoms with orange centers appear in foot-long spikes in summer and fall, attracting butterflies with their fragrance.   AREAS: C D E G I J

BURNINGBUSH See *Euonymus*
BUTTERFLY BUSH See *Buddleia*

CALYCANTHUS
C. floridus (sweet shrub, Carolina allspice)
Used individually or massed in shrub borders, the dense 4- to 9-foot sweet shrub in summer is a mound of shiny corrugated leaves and 2-inch reddish brown blossoms. The flowers and leaves are fragrant, as is the bark. The leaves turn yellow in fall.   AREAS: B C D E G I J

CARAGANA (PEA TREE)
C. arborescens (Siberian pea tree)
The Siberian pea tree has slender, upright branches, grows to 15 to 20 feet and is suitable for screens or hedges in dry, windy, sandy areas. Small yellow flowers appear amid fern-like leaves in early spring.   AREAS: A B C F H I

CAROLINA ALLSPICE See *Calycanthus*

ORANGE-EYED BUTTERFLY BUSH
Buddleia davidii

Key letters refer to growing areas shown on map, page 154.   113

JAPANESE QUINCE
Chaenomeles japonica

NOTCUTT SMOKE TREE
Cotinus coggygria 'Notcutt'

CRANBERRY COTONEASTER
Cotoneaster apiculata

CARYOPTERIS
Caryopteris varieties (bluebeard)
These rounded shrubs make excellent borders, grow rapidly to 2 to 4 feet and bear clusters of small blue or lavender flowers that provide a rare autumn display. They thrive in dry soil. Among the most popular types are 'Blue Mist' and 'Heavenly Blue.'   AREAS: ☐ C D ☐ G ☐ I ☐

CHAENOMELES, also called CYDONIA (QUINCE)
Chaenomeles species and varieties (flowering quince)
The most popular species of flowering quince are *C. japonica* and *C. speciosa;* they are used as hedges or accent plants primarily because of their spectacular early bloom. Some blossom in February in southern areas, producing white, pink or red flowers that resemble apple blossoms and grow in loose clusters of two to four. The aromatic, greenish yellow fruit that follows makes a tasty jelly. Varieties include low, spreading types under 3 feet tall and 5- to 6-foot upright plants.   AREAS: B C D E ☐ G ☐ I J

CHASTE TREE See *Vitex*
CHERRY See *Prunus*
CINQUEFOIL See *Potentilla*
CORNELIAN CHERRY See *Cornus*

CORNUS (DOGWOOD)
(See also Deciduous trees, page 103.)
C. alba sibirica (Siberian dogwood)
This ornamental shrub grows rapidly into a 7- to 9-foot mound usually planted by itself for dramatic color: yellowish white flower clusters in spring, bluish white berries in summer, dark red leaves in fall and bright coral-red branches in winter.   AREAS: A B C ☐ ☐ F G H I ☐

C. mas (Cornelian cherry)
Like the Siberian dogwood, the Cornelian cherry is best planted alone. Tiny feathery clusters of yellow blossoms clothe the upright spreading boughs in very early spring. Summer brings a deep red, cherrylike fruit that can be made into a delicious preserve. The foliage turns red in fall. If not pruned to shrub dimensions, it may reach a tree-like height of 20 to 25 feet.   AREAS: ☐ B C D ☐ ☐ ☐ I ☐

COTINUS, also called RHUS COTINUS
C. coggygria 'Notcutt' (smoke tree, smokebush)
The spectacular smoke tree is enveloped in plumelike reddish purple blossoms in late summer and fall. The effect of the autumn foliage, in hues of yellow, orange and scarlet, is heightened by the fluffy mass of the dry panicles that cling until late in the season. Slow growing, the smoke tree may grow 15 feet tall and equally wide; it does best in full sun and well-drained soil.   AREAS: ☐ C D ☐ G ☐ I ☐

COTONEASTER
Gracefully arching branches adorn the many species of cotoneaster, which range from ground covers less than a foot high to tall shrubs of 15 feet or more. All bear small white or pinkish purple blossoms in late spring, red or black berries in summer, and tolerate seashore conditions. Tall-growing species make fine informal hedges or screen plantings. *(See also Broad-leaved evergreen shrubs, page 136.)*

C. apiculata (cranberry cotoneaster)
The prostrate branches of this 2- to 3-foot shrub are best displayed at the top of a wall or in a massed planting. In spring, tiny pink flowers contrast with dark, shiny leaves; showy, cranberry-sized red berries follow. In fall the leaves turn scarlet.   AREAS: ☐ B C ☐ ☐ ☐ ☐ I J

C. divaricata (spreading cotoneaster)
The spreading cotoneaster grows 5 to 6 feet high and often spreads 8 to 10 feet. In late spring, pinkish clusters of minuscule flowers bloom, followed by tiny red berries relished by chipmunks and birds.　AREAS: | | |C|D|E| |G| |I|J|

CRANBERRY BUSH See *Viburnum*
CYDONIA See *Chaenomeles*

CYTISUS
Cytisus species and varieties (broom)
Brooms are fast-growing shrubs with slender, upright or trailing, bright green branches that are attractive even without foliage. Once used to make sweeping brooms, broom grows from 6 inches to 9 feet in height depending on the variety. In spring, tiny dark green leaves are buried under masses of pealike yellow blossoms (some varieties are red, purple or white). Brooms do well in the poorest soils and resist disease and pests.　AREAS: | | |C|D| | | | |I|J|

DAPHNE
(See also Broad-leaved evergreen shrubs, page 137.)
D. mezereum (February daphne)
Planted in a sunny protected site, this low (to 3 feet), upright-growing shrub provides an effective contrast to winter evergreens when it sprouts its tiny, highly fragrant, rosy lavender blossoms in early spring. Poisonous red berries appear in June.　AREAS: | |B|C|D| |F| | |I| |

DEUTZIA
Deutzia species and varieties
These fast-growing, profusely blooming shrubs reach 3 to 8 feet and have dense, dark green foliage; clusters of white or pink bell-like flowers cover the plants in spring or early summer. Deutzias tolerate light shade and dry soil and resist pests and diseases.　AREAS: | |B|C|D|E| |G| |I|J|

DOGWOOD See *Cornus*

ELAEAGNUS
(See also Deciduous trees, page 104, and Broad-leaved evergreen shrubs, page 137.)
E. multiflorus, also called *E. longipes* (cherry elaeagnus)
The sturdy mound-shaped cherry elaeagnus, which grows rapidly to heights of 6 to 9 feet, is often used for hedges, particularly in windy, sunny locations. Small, fragrant, yellowish white flowers open in spring, and are partly obscured by the dense, dark green leaves, which have silvery undersides. Tart but edible red-orange cherrylike berries follow the flowers.　AREAS: | |B|C|D| | |H| | | |

ENKIANTHUS
E. campanulatus (redvein enkianthus)
The upright redvein enkianthus, which grows 5 to 10 feet tall, bears pendulous clusters of bell-shaped, yellow or light orange flowers in spring; in fall the leaves turn scarlet. Named for tiny red lines on its blossoms, it tolerates full sunlight and light shade and thrives in acid humus-rich soil.　AREAS: | |B|C|D| | | | |I| |

EUONYMUS
(See also Broad-leaved evergreen shrubs, page 138, Ground covers, page 146, and Vines, page 150.)
E. alata compacta (dwarf winged euonymus, dwarf burning bush)
Useful as a compact, unclipped hedge or accent plant, this shrub grows 4 to 5 feet high in a dense mound. Its common names refer to the winglike ridges that line its branches

Key letters refer to growing areas shown on map, page 154.

SLENDER DEUTZIA
Deutzia gracilis

REDVEIN ENKIANTHUS
Enkianthus campanulatus

DWARF WINGED EUONYMUS, DWARF BURNING BUSH
Euonymus alata compacta

LYNWOOD FORSYTHIA
Forsythia intermedia 'Lynwood'

RUBY DOT ROSE OF SHARON
Hibiscus syriacus 'Ruby Dot'

COMMON BIGLEAF HYDRANGEA, HOUSE HYDRANGEA
Hydrangea macrophylla

and the spectacular red color of its leaves and capsulelike scarlet fruit in fall. AREAS: B C F G H I

FORSYTHIA
Forsythia species and varieties
Among the most popular and earliest-blooming garden shrubs, forsythias produce their loosely arching or trailing sprays of yellow flowers in March or early April. Most forsythias grow 6 to 9 feet high and equally wide and can be used singly or in informal hedges. A small variety, 'Arnold Dwarf,' grows 3 to 4 feet tall; it makes a good, high, ground cover but produces few flowers. Forsythias tolerate light shade, thrive in all but extremely dry soils and are disease and pest resistant. AREAS: C D G I

HIBISCUS
(See also Broad-leaved evergreen shrubs, page 139.)
H. syriacus (rose of Sharon, shrub althea)
The rose of Sharon is valued for its late-flowering habit, which brings color to gardens after other shrubs have finished blooming. In mid to late summer its upright branches sprout a profusion of 3- to 4-inch blossoms, ranging from whitish pink to reddish purple. Fast growing and dense, it may reach 10 to 15 feet. AREAS: C D E G I J

HONEYSUCKLE See *Lonicera*

HYDRANGEA
(See also Vines, page 150.)
H. macrophylla, also called *H. hortensis*
(common bigleaf hydrangea, house hydrangea)
Planted as a single ornamental shrub or massed in borders, the common hydrangea grows 3 to 6 feet tall and equally broad, producing spectacular globular flower clusters up to 10 inches across. Flower color varies according to the soil: alkaline soil produces pinkish blossoms, acid soil produces bluish ones (white-flowered varieties are not affected by soil acidity). AREAS: D E I J

H. paniculata grandiflora (peegee hydrangea)
This dense shrub, which can grow to 20 feet or more unless pruned, affords ample privacy as a screening plant. Large, white, conical flower clusters bloom in late summer; after a few weeks they turn pinkish and often survive in dried form through the winter. AREAS: B C F G H I

KOLKWITZIA
K. amabilis (beauty bush)
The fountain-like appearance of the tall (up to 10 feet), spreading beauty bush makes it an ideal decorative plant used singly or in borders. Clusters of pink flowers blanket the shrub in spring, obscuring the gray-green leaves. Autumn brings reddish foliage. AREAS: B C D F G H I J

LIGUSTRUM (PRIVET)
Attractive glossy leaves, tolerance of poor soils and resistance to pests and diseases make the upright, fast-growing privets valuable hedge and screen plants. Small white flowers, borne in clusters in summer, are followed by blue or black berries that cling through the winter. *(See also Broad-leaved evergreen shrubs, page 140.)*

L. amurense (Amur privet)
L. ovalifolium (California privet)
These species, similar except for hardiness, can grow to 15 feet tall; in milder climates they are semievergreen.

L. amurense	AREAS:	B C D E F G H I
L. ovalifolium	AREAS:	C D E G I J

LILAC See *Syringa*

LONICERA
(See also Broad-leaved evergreen shrubs, page 141, and Vines, page 151.)
Lonicera species and varieties (honeysuckle)
Honeysuckles, many but not all of which have exceedingly fragrant blossoms, are free-flowering shrubs that make effective screen plantings or informal hedges. Clusters of small trumpet-shaped flowers—white, pink, red, purple or yellow depending on the variety—appear in early summer and are followed by clusters of red, white, yellow, blue or black berries that attract birds. The plants are tolerant of poor soils and may grow 6 to 10 or more feet tall in sunlit locations.   AREAS: B C D E F G H I J

MOCK ORANGE See *Philadelphus*

PAEONIA (PEONY)
P. suffruticosa (tree peony)
The tree peony grows slowly to 4 to 5 feet tall, often spreading 6 to 8 feet across. Its white, red, yellow, pink or purple blossoms, up to a full foot across, appear in spring against large blue-green leaves and are so heavy they often need support. Tree peonies do best in rich well-drained soil and light shade.   AREAS: C D I

PEA TREE See *Caragana*
PEONY See *Paeonia*

PHILADELPHUS
Philadelphus species and varieties (mock orange)
For two weeks in late spring or early summer, most varieties of mock orange bear a profusion of fragrant white flowers resembling orange blossoms. Single- and double-flowered varieties are available, varying from upright to arching in growth habit. Average height is 6 to 8 feet, although some varieties grow to 3 feet or 12 feet. Mock oranges grow in most soils.   AREAS: B C D F G H I J

POTENTILLA (CINQUEFOIL)
P. fruticosa varieties (bush cinquefoil)
The most common varieties of the hardy bush cinquefoil are slow-growing rounded shrubs from 2 to 4 feet high that bear small yellow or white flowers all summer and can be used to enhance sunny spots near the house or in the forefront of a shrub border. Named for their tiny five-leaflet leaves, the plants grow in poor, dry soil and resist diseases and pests.   AREAS: A B C F H I

PRIVET See *Ligustrum*

PRUNUS (ALMOND, CHERRY)
(See also Deciduous trees, page 109, and Broad-leaved evergreen shrubs, page 143.)
P. glandulosa, double-flowered varieties
(dwarf flowering almond)
Often used as accent plants near deciduous or evergreen borders, these shrubs provide countless clusters of pomponlike white or pink blossoms as the narrow, dark green leaves unfold in early spring. Plants grow rapidly as low, dense mounds to a height of 3 to 5 feet. Double-flowered varieties do not bear fruit.   AREAS: B C D F G H I

P. tomentosa (Manchu or Nanking cherry)
A good hedge or accent plant, the Manchu cherry is especially decorative in early spring, when red-stamened white blossoms precede the oval, dark green leaves. The

Key letters refer to growing areas shown on map, page 154.

BEAUTY BUSH
Kolkwitzia amabilis

TREE PEONY
Paeonia suffruticosa

GLACIER MOCK ORANGE
Philadelphus virginalis 'Glacier'

plants grow upright 5 to 9 feet tall and often spread as wide. The midsummer crop of cherries may be eaten fresh or made into jelly or jam. AREAS: A B C ▢ ▢ F ▢ H I ▢ ▢

QUINCE See *Chaenomeles*

RHODODENDRON (RHODODENDRON, AZALEA)
Deciduous azaleas and rhododendrons, like evergreen ones *(page 143)*, are prized for their brilliant spring display of blossoms and for their deep green foliage, which often turns yellow to crimson in fall. All species require acid, organically rich soil and prefer light shade.

R. calendulaceum, also called *Azalea calendulacea*
(flame azalea)
Named for the blazing orange, yellow or scarlet color of its blossoms, the flame azalea has 2- to 3½-inch-long leaves; it usually grows 4 to 10 feet tall and can be used as a single ornament or in screens. AREAS: ▢ ▢ C D ▢ ▢ ▢ I ▢ ▢

R. 'Exbury hybrids' (Exbury azalea)
Hybridized to produce large (3-inch) blossoms in combinations of yellow, salmon, pink, red and white, these shrubs usually grow 4 to 5 feet tall. The leaves are 2 to 3 inches long. AREAS: ▢ ▢ ▢ D ▢ ▢ ▢ I ▢ ▢

R. mucronulatum (Korean rhododendron)
This rhododendron blossoms at the first hint of warm weather, covering itself with rosy purple flowers against 3-inch-long leaves. Plants may become 5 to 6 feet tall and should be planted in shade so premature flowers will not be nipped by frost. AREAS: ▢ B C D ▢ ▢ ▢ I ▢

R. schlippenbachii, also called *Azalea schlippenbachii*
(royal azalea)
One of the loveliest and largest azaleas, this pink-blossomed shrub, whose flowers are 3 inches in diameter, normally grows 6 to 8 feet tall but may become 15 feet tall in a favored location. Leaves are up to 5 inches long with pale undersides. AREAS: ▢ B C D ▢ ▢ ▢ I ▢

RHUS COTINUS See *Cotinus*

ROSA (ROSE)
R. rugosa and varieties (rugosa rose)
Fragrant purplish red or white 3-inch flowers, brick-red hips and thorny stems make this rose, which thrives at seashores, a handsome, effective barrier hedge. Most blossoms open in early summer, but some flowers appear until fall. The fruit that follows can be made into rose-hip jelly or jam. Bushes grow 5 to 6 feet tall and spread to make large clumps. The dense, dark green wrinkled foliage turns orange in fall. AREAS: A B C D ▢ F ▢ H I J

ROSE OF SHARON See *Hibiscus*
SHRUB ALTHEA See *Hibiscus*
SMOKE TREE See *Cotinus*
SNOWBALL See *Viburnum*
SNOWBERRY See *Symphoricarpos*

SPIRAEA
Spiraea species and varieties (spirea, bridalwreath)
Tiny white, pink or red flowers, which appear in clusters on graceful arching or upright branches in late spring, make the fast-growing spireas popular ornaments or screens. Most species range from 2 to 8 feet tall; a few become 10 to 12 feet tall. All thrive in almost any soil, in sun or light shade. AREAS: ▢ B C D E F G H I J

EXBURY AZALEA
Rhododendron 'Exbury Hybrid'

ROYAL AZALEA
Rhododendron schlippenbachii (Azalea schlippenbachii)

RUGOSA ROSE
Rosa rugosa

SWEET SHRUB See *Calycanthus*

SYMPHORICARPOS

S. albus laevigatus, also called *S. racemosus* (snowberry)
Shrub borders or open areas suit the spreading ornamental snowberry, since its arching outer branches often touch the ground. Tiny pink flowers are almost hidden by the dark green leaves in mid-June; two months later the branches are weighted down by clusters of waxy white berries. These fast-growing plants, which may reach 6 feet in height, thrive in dry soil and partial shade.   AREAS: B C | | F G H I J

SYRINGA (LILAC)

(See also Deciduous trees, page 111.)
S. vulgaris hybrids (French hybrid lilacs)
Effective as hedge plants, screens or solitary shrubs, the French hybrid forms of the common lilac are among the most popular flowering shrubs in America. In midspring, huge clusters of fragrant lilac, violet, blue, pink, magenta, purple, cream or white blossoms—depending on the variety —adorn branches dense with dark green foliage. The shrubs are hardy, tolerate most soils and grow upright to a height of 10 to 20 feet.   AREAS: B C | | F G H I |

TAMARIX (TAMARISK)

Tamarisks are open, feathery-branched shrubs that bear spiky clusters of tiny pink flowers in midsummer. Unusually rugged plants, they do well in seashore locations.

T. odessana (Odessa tamarisk)
T. pentandra (five-stamen tamarisk)
Both species are effective as screens or single plants, differing only in hardiness and in height: the five-stamen type may reach a straggly 15 feet, whereas the Odessa stays under 6 feet.   *T. odessana*   AREAS: B C | F G | I J
            T. pentandra   AREAS: A B C | | F G H I J

VIBURNUM

Spreading, profusely flowering, highly ornamental plants, the three viburnums listed below are best appreciated when they are planted singly. They do best in moist rich soil and rarely require pruning. *(See also Broad-leaved evergreen shrubs, page 145.)*

V. carlcephalum (fragrant snowball)
This hybrid fragrant snowball, which grows 6 to 9 feet tall, bears 4- to 5-inch globular clusters of clove-scented white flowers in late spring. The tiny dark green leaves turn bright red in fall.   AREAS: | C D | G | I J

V. plicatum, also called *V. tomentosum sterile*
(Japanese snowball)
Growing 5 to 7 feet tall with wide-spreading horizontal branches, this species gives a layered effect, especially in late spring, when spherical white flowers appear. Fall turns the leaves a deep purplish red.   AREAS: B C D | G | I J

V. trilobum, also called *V. americanum*
(American cranberry bush)
Although the American cranberry bush can be used as a background screen plant—it may grow 12 feet tall—it is often more effective as a single shrub. Its branches grow quickly and in all directions, creating a slightly haphazard appearance, and bear flat-topped white flower clusters in spring. In fall, red foliage accompanies heavy clusters of tart but edible red berries, which look and taste like cranberries. Unless picked for jelly or eaten by birds, the berries remain through the winter.   AREAS: A B C | F | H I J

Key letters refer to growing areas shown on map, page 154.

BRIDALWREATH SPIREA
Spiraea prunifolia

VICTOR LEMOINE LILAC
Syringa vulgaris 'Victor Lemoine'

FRAGRANT SNOWBALL
Viburnum carlcephalum

VITEX

V. agnus-castus (chaste tree)
This fast-growing shrub can be used alone or for screening or borders. Its long spikes of lavender flowers bloom in late summer, and its star-shaped leaves are aromatic. In frost-free areas, plants grow as high as 15 to 20 feet but elsewhere reach 6 to 9 feet. AREAS: | | |D|E| | |I|J|

WEIGELA

Weigela species and varieties (weigela)
Used singly or in hedges, weigelas are valued primarily for their trumpet-shaped, white, pink or red blossoms, which appear in late spring. The fast-growing shrubs may reach 9 to 12 feet, but are often half that high. Some varieties have colorful fall foliage. AREAS: | |C|D| |F| | |I| |

Evergreen trees

The major value of evergreens is implicit in their name; they furnish constant color and mass, providing individual ornaments, privacy screens or windbreaks in all seasons. Not all species remain green, however; some turn red, bronze or purple in fall and winter. Some species are semievergreen, bearing their leaves year round only in mild climates.

Evergreen trees are classified into two groups, those that have narrow, needle- or scalelike leaves and bear cones (from which they derive their alternate name, "conifer") and those that have broad, often glossy, leaves, frequently augmented by attractive flowers and fruit. While most narrow-leaved types—firs, hemlocks, spruces—grow well into far northern areas, most broad-leaved evergreens—southern magnolias, eucalyptuses, evergreen oaks—are not as hardy.

The growth rate of evergreens, like other plants, depends on species, age, conditions and length of growing season. When young, pines in the South, for example, often put on 3 to 5 feet a year, while pines suitable to the North may grow 1½ to 2 feet; each is fast growing for its region. Slow-growing varieties such as dwarf pines put on less than a foot a year.

Narrow-leaved evergreen trees

ABIES (FIR)

A. concolor (white fir, concolor fir)
Tall and pyramidal, white firs make handsome individual trees, privacy screens and windbreaks, growing 30 to 50 feet tall in gardens. They have flat, bluish green needles and upright cones up to 5 inches long. White firs are the most tolerant of air pollution, and are among the most heat and drought resistant. AREAS: | |B|C| | |F|G|H|I| |

ARAUCARIA

A. excelsa (Norfolk Island pine)
Although wild trees become 200 feet high, garden plants usually grow to 50 feet tall and 20 feet wide at the base, with horizontal or drooping, dark green, fernlike branchlets forming a pyramidal outline. Older trees bear 3- to 6-inch, nearly globular cones. AREAS: | | | |E| | | |J|

AUSTRALIAN PINE See *Casuarina*
BEEFWOOD See *Casuarina*
CALOCEDRUS DECURRENS See *Libocedrus*

CASUARINA

C. equisetifolia (horsetail beefwood, Australian pine)
Not true conifers but similar in appearance, horsetail beefwoods make good screens and windbreaks; their slender,

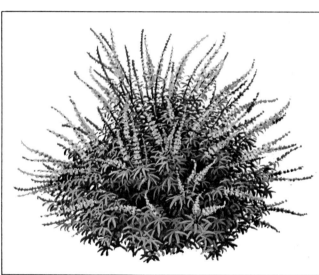

CHASTE TREE
Vitex agnus-castus

drooping branches can be pruned attractively and their far-reaching roots will prevent erosion of banks even close to salt water. Trees are fast growing and may reach 60 or 70 feet with a spread of 20 feet; they thrive in moist salty soil and withstand wind.   AREAS: [| | E | | | J]

CEDAR See *Cedrus*

CEDRUS (CEDAR)
Cedars are tall pyramidal trees that reach 60 to 100 feet in height and as much as 40 feet in breadth. They have tufted clusters of short stiff needles and blunt-ended, 3- to 4-inch cones. They do best in rich well-drained soil.

C. atlantica glauca (blue Atlas cedar)
One of the bluest evergreens, this stiff-branched upright tree makes a handsome accent.   AREAS: [| |C|D| |G| |I|J]

C. deodara (deodar cedar)
The deodar cedar is a majestic evergreen for individual planting. It bears soft gray-green needles on gracefully pendant branches; even the tip of the tree arches over in the same characteristic curve.   AREAS: [| | |D|E| | |I|J]

CEDAR, INCENSE See *Libocedrus*
CEDAR, PORT ORFORD See *Chamaecyparis*

CEPHALOTAXUS (PLUM YEW)
C. harringtonia, also called *C. drupacea*
(Japanese plum yew)
A small wide-spreading tree with a broad, round head and dark green needles, this tree makes a good screen or hedge. It grows slowly to about 30 feet and thrives in moist acid soil and light shade. Older trees bear inedible red fruits that resemble plums.   AREAS: [| | |D|E| | |I|J]

CHAMAECYPARIS (FALSE CYPRESS)
(See also Narrow-leaved evergreen shrubs, page 131.)
C. lawsoniana and varieties
(Lawson false cypress, Port Orford cedar)
These trees grow 60 feet or more with dense branches close to the ground and resemble cypresses *(below)* except for minor differences in cones and foliage. They can be planted singly or in screens, respond well to shearing, but need moist soil and protection from winds. The scarab false cypress *(C. lawsoniana allumii),* a columnar variety, has steel-blue foliage.   AREAS: [| |C|D| | | |I|J]

CRYPTOMERIA
C. japonica (cryptomeria)
Cryptomeria bears its blue-green needles close to slender stems, which are grouped together at the ends of the branches. The reddish brown bark sheds in long strips, and in cooler areas the foliage turns bronze in winter. Trees may grow 100 feet tall but require moist soil and protection from drying winds. Cryptomerias make massive single ornaments in a landscape.   AREAS: [| |C|D| | | |I|J]

CUPRESSUS (CYPRESS)
Cypresses make good individual ornaments or screening trees, but most species cannot stand high winds. They grow upright and have shedding bark and aromatic scalelike leaves set close together on twisted ropelike branches.

C. arizonica (Arizona cypress)
A fast-growing drought-resistant tree, this species reaches 35 to 40 feet with a spread of 15 to 20 feet. It has light gray-blue foliage and reddish bark.   AREAS: [| | | | |G| |J]

Key letters refer to growing areas shown on map, page 154.

WHITE FIR, CONCOLOR FIR
Abies concolor

BLUE ATLAS CEDAR
Cedrus atlantica glauca

MOERHEIM COLORADO SPRUCE
Picea pungens moerheimii

EASTERN WHITE PINE
Pinus strobus

C. sempervirens stricta (Italian cypress)
These columnar, dark green cypresses are highly ornamental. Familiar to travelers in southern Europe, the trees grow from 20 to 80 feet tall in this country and thrive in both dry and moist soils. AREAS: |_|_|D|E|_|_|J|

CYPRESS See *Cupressus*
CYPRESS, FALSE See *Chamaecyparis*
DOUGLAS FIR See *Pseudotsuga*
FALSE CYPRESS See *Chamaecyparis*
FIR See *Abies*
FIR, DOUGLAS See *Pseudotsuga*
HEMLOCK See *Tsuga*
INCENSE CEDAR See *Libocedrus*

LIBOCEDRUS (INCENSE CEDAR)

L. decurrens, also called *Calocedrus decurrens*
(California incense cedar)
A tall, columnar or narrowly pyramidal tree, the California incense cedar grows to heights of 50 to 130 feet. Flat sprays of lustrous, fragrant, bright green needles are borne on short upright branches covered with cinnamon-red bark. These trees make fine accents; set in rows, they form tough windbreaks. AREAS: |_|C|D|E|_|_|I|J|

NORFOLK ISLAND PINE See *Araucaria*

PICEA (SPRUCE)

Spruces are handsome ornamental trees and many species are suitable for screens, windbreaks or individual planting. The branches of most species grow in regular whorls or circles, assuming the pyramidal habit that is associated with Christmas trees. Spruces require sun and grow best in moist well-drained soil. They thrive in cold climates and tolerate wind.

P. abies, also called *P. excelsa,* and varieties
(Norway spruce)
The Norway spruce is a decorative, fast-growing, pyramidal tree that may attain a height of 75 to 100 feet. Its light brown cones, up to 6 inches long, are borne high on older trees. Columnar, weeping and dwarf varieties abound; the last are particularly suited to use in rock gardens and lower plantings near houses because of their extremely slow growth. AREAS:|A|B|C|_|_|F|_|H|I|

P. glauca densata (Black Hills spruce)
A broadly pyramidal, compact tree that eventually reaches 40 to 50 feet, the slow-growing Black Hills spruce retains its lower branches throughout its long life. It is handsome alone and forms fine screens or windbreaks, as it tolerates crowding, heavy pruning and severe winter winds as well as heat and drought. AREAS:|A|B|C|_|_|F|_|H|I|

P. pungens and varieties (Colorado spruce)
Dense, erect trees with regularly spaced branches, the Colorado spruces have foliage that varies from a silvery blue-green to a deep purplish blue. With the exception of one "weeping" variety, the branches spring at right angles from the trunk. The intense blue of certain varieties like the Moerheim spruce *(P. pungens moerheimii)* makes them focal points in any landscape, so they should be located with some care. AREAS:|A|B|C|_|_|F|_|H|I|

PINE See *Pinus*
PINE, AUSTRALIAN See *Casuarina*
PINE, NORFOLK ISLAND See *Araucaria*
PINE, UMBRELLA See *Sciadopitys*

122

PINUS (PINE)

The pines, the largest genus of conifers, include species and varieties suitable to almost every area and use. Young pines make fast-growing screens or windbreaks; older trees, pruned high, provide protection for shade-loving broad-leaved evergreens such as rhododendrons and camellias. *(See also Narrow-leaved evergreen shrubs, page 133.)*

P. canariensis (Canary Island pine)
The fast-growing Canary Island pine reaches heights of 70 to 80 feet in dry, even rocky, soil. A narrow tree with light green needles when young, it assumes a tiered pyramidal shape and darker foliage as it grows. It is a handsome accent tree because of the extreme length (9 to 12 inches) of its pendant needles. AREAS: | | | E | | | J

P. caribaea (slash pine, swamp pine, Cuban pine)
The slash pine is fast growing, often putting on more than 3 feet a year; its irregularly set, horizontal branches form a compact, round crown some 15 to 20 feet wide atop a tree that may reach 70 to 100 feet. Slash pines grow best in moist soil. AREAS: | | | E | | | |

P. halepensis (Aleppo pine)
The Aleppo pine's short branches reach upward at an acute angle when the tree is young, but spread outward with age. Fast growing in nearly any well-drained soil—a 6-inch seedling may reach 15 feet in four years—the trees resist drought and heat and make fine screens or windbreaks, especially in seaside locations. AREAS: | | | | | | | J

P. ponderosa scopulorum (Rocky Mountain yellow pine)
A hardy variety of the stately ponderosa, this stiff-needled tree displays the pines' familiar pyramidal shape when young, and may grow to 75 feet or more. It is suited to windbreaks and screens and is splendid planted alone if given ample room to develop. AREAS: | | | | F G H I |

P. strobus and varieties (eastern white pine)
The eastern white pine is broadly pyramidal, with soft blue-green needles and long slim cones, and often grows at the rate of 1 to 2 feet per year when young, attaining 50 to 75 feet. It is useful in screens and windbreaks or when planted singly or in groups, and can be kept small for years by proper pruning. Columnar and weeping varieties are used as accent trees, and there are also slow-growing, rounded dwarf varieties. AREAS: A B C D | | H I |

P. sylvestris (Scotch pine, Scots pine)
The Scotch pine is a full, pyramidal tree with stiff blue-green needles when young; in older trees the branches, more loosely spaced and slightly drooping, allow glimpses of orange-red bark. This fast-growing pine, which often has a picturesque crooked trunk, is extremely hardy and tolerant of wet or dry soil. The trees can be pruned to maintain their thick growth. AREAS: A B C | | F | H I |

P. thunbergii (Japanese black pine)
On the rainy Northwest coast this handsome species grows swiftly to a height of 80 to 100 feet, its spreading branches forming a broad, conical silhouette. In cold or dry areas with sandy soil, it grows more slowly, rarely exceeding 20 feet, and assumes the picturesque irregularity of old trees in Japan. It is suited to seashore hedges or windbreaks, as it stands wind and takes to pruning. It also grows well in tubs as a bonsai plant. AREAS: | B C D | G | I J

PLUM YEW See *Cephalotaxus*

JAPANESE BLACK PINE
Pinus thunbergii

Key letters refer to growing areas shown on map, page 154.

CANADA HEMLOCK
Tsuga canadensis

PODOCARPUS

P. macrophyllus and varieties (yew podocarpus)
The yew podocarpus grows in a broad, columnar shape, seldom reaching more than 20 feet in height, with horizontally spreading branches and drooping branchlets thickly covered with needle-shaped leaves 3 to 4 inches long. The trees can be pruned to make dense hedges, screens or windbreaks. A smaller variety, *P. macrophyllus makii*, grows 6 to 12 feet tall.   AREAS: | | |D|E| | |I|J| |

PORT ORFORD CEDAR See *Chamaecyparis*

PSEUDOTSUGA

P. menziesii, also called *P. taxifolia, P. douglasii*
(Douglas fir)
Familiar as a Christmas tree, the Douglas fir has slender graceful branches clothed with soft blue-green needles and grows 40 to 100 feet tall in home landscapes. It holds its lower branches well, responds to shearing and is a good choice for hedges or screens as well as for individual plantings. The trees will grow in a wide variety of soils, but prefer a moist well-drained site.   AREAS: |B|C| | | | |H|I| |

SCIADOPITYS

S. verticillata (umbrella pine)
The umbrella pine's short slender branches form a dark compact pyramid that seldom exceeds 25 feet. The whorled arrangement of its long glossy needles, which are set like umbrella ribs at the ends of the stems, accounts for its common name. It is a connoisseur's tree, worthy of the finest landscape setting.   AREAS: | |C|D| | | |I|J| |

SPRUCE See *Picea*

TSUGA (HEMLOCK)

Hemlocks, handsome trees with cinnamon-red bark and a profusion of small pendulous cones, are moderate to fast growing and prefer full sun, although they tolerate shade. The dark green, needlelike foliage is soft to the touch and thrives on pruning, making hemlocks among the finest plants for hedges and screens. Easy to transplant, they flourish with ample moisture and shelter from wind.

T. canadensis and varieties (Canada hemlock)
Dense and pyramidal, with graceful downswept branches, the Canada hemlock makes a splendid landscape ornament. If allowed to grow naturally, it can reach heights of 50 feet or more in gardens, with a 25-foot spread, but it can be topped and pruned to serve in hedges or screens. Sargent's weeping hemlock is a fountain-shaped slow-growing variety that spreads up to 20 feet across but seldom exceeds 10 feet in height; it is suited to large rock gardens or containers on a patio when young.   AREAS: |B|C| | | | | |I| |

T. caroliniana (Carolina hemlock)
Small, neat and compact (15 to 40 feet), the Carolina hemlock is a good choice for city planting because of its tolerance of pollution.   AREAS: | |C|D| | | | |I| |

T. heterophylla
(western hemlock, mountain hemlock)
This fast-growing symmetrical tree can reach 50 feet or more in moist soils. It is a fine choice for individual planting, screens or hedges.   AREAS: | | | | | | | |I| |

UMBRELLA PINE See *Sciadopitys*
YEW, PLUM See *Cephalotaxus*
YEW PODOCARPUS See *Podocarpus*

Broad-leaved evergreen trees

ACACIA

Acacias are prized for their speedy growth—up to 25 feet in six years—and for their ornamental, sometimes fragrant, blossoms. The acacias below make good patio trees and quick-growing screens. They can be pruned to grow as shrubs.

A. baileyana (Cootamundra wattle, Bailey acacia)
This vigorous species grows 20 to 30 feet tall as a graceful, spreading tree with feathery foliage. It blooms early, from January to March, and is covered with large clusters of globular yellow flowers.　　AREAS:⬚⬚⬚⬚⬚⬚⬚⬚|J|

A. longifolia floribunda (gossamer Sydney wattle)
This attractive variety produces many fluffy, pale yellow, ball-like flowers in February and March, and occasional flowers throughout the year.　　AREAS:⬚⬚⬚⬚⬚⬚⬚⬚|J|

ACHRAS

A. sapota (sapodilla)
The long glossy leaves and spreading branches of the oval-shaped sapodilla provide shade; its tough wood, preference for sandy soil and immunity to salt winds make it a suitable plant for seashore sites in southern Florida. The tree grows 35 to 40 feet tall and bears small white flowers. Its large, russet-colored, egg-shaped fruits taste like pears and can be made into sherbet.　　AREAS:⬚⬚⬚|E|⬚⬚⬚⬚

AGONIS

A. flexuosa (willow myrtle, peppermint tree)
This medium-to-fast-growing shade tree reaches 20 to 40 feet. It has spreading, weeping branches heavily clothed in slender, bright green leaves, which are copper red when young. When crushed, the leaves smell like peppermint. In early summer the tree bears dense round clusters of small, fragrant white flowers. It thrives in light dry soil and sea-side locations.　　AREAS:⬚⬚⬚⬚⬚⬚⬚⬚|J|

ASH See *Fraxinus*
AUSTRALIAN BEECH See *Eucalyptus*
AUSTRALIAN UMBRELLA TREE See *Brassaia*

BAUHINIA

B. blakeana (Hong Kong orchid tree)
Dark green leaves and large, fragrant, orchidlike flowers make this tree, which grows 20 to 25 feet tall, a good choice for patios or as an accent plant. The blossoms, often ranging from pink to crimson in the same flowers, appear from October through March.　　AREAS:⬚⬚⬚|E|⬚⬚|J|

BAY, BULL See *Magnolia*
BAY, CALIFORNIA See *Umbellularia*
BAY, SWEET See *Magnolia*
BEECH, AUSTRALIAN See *Eucalyptus*
BOTTLE TREE See *Brachychiton*
BOTTLEBRUSH See *Callistemon*

BRACHYCHITON

B. populneum, also called *Sterculia diversifolia* (bottle tree)
Named for the bottlelike swelling of its trunk, this slow-growing tree, which reaches 30 to 50 feet, makes a good screen or windbreak, shade or street tree. Clusters of small, bell-shaped, white flowers appear in late spring and are followed by brown, woody fruit pods up to 3 inches long and shaped like tiny canoes.　　AREAS:⬚⬚⬚⬚⬚⬚⬚⬚|J|

Key letters refer to growing areas shown on map, page 154.

COOTAMUNDRA WATTLE, BAILEY ACACIA
Acacia baileyana

HONG KONG ORCHID TREE
Bauhinia blakeana

CAMPHOR TREE
Cinnamomum camphora

BRASSAIA

B. actinophylla, also called *Schefflera actinophylla*
(Australian umbrella tree, Queensland umbrella tree,
octopus tree)
Huge, fingerlike, shiny green leaves, spread out atop long
stems like umbrellas, make this tree an attractive ornament. It grows rapidly to 20 to 30 feet tall and bears long
upright clusters of greenish yellow, pink or dark red flowers in late spring or early autumn, followed by small purple
berries. The outspread flower spikes account for the name
octopus tree. The species is recommended for planting only
in frost-free areas. AREAS: E J

BULL BAY See *Magnolia*
CAJEPUT TREE See *Melaleuca*
CALIFORNIA BAY See *Umbellularia*
CALIFORNIA LAUREL See *Umbellularia*

CALLISTEMON

C. viminalis (weeping bottlebrush)
A highly ornamental tree, the bottlebrush grows rapidly to
a height of 20 to 30 feet. It has open foliage and cascading
branches that in summer are filled with bright red blossoms resembling bottlebrushes; occasional flowers appear
throughout the year. AREAS: E J

CAMPHOR TREE See *Cinnamomum*
CAROB See *Ceratonia*
CARROTWOOD See *Cupaniopsis*

CERATONIA

C. siliqua (carob, St. John's bread)
This handsome rounded tree grows slowly to 40 to 50 feet
in height and breadth. Small red flowers appear in fall,
and the shiny, dark green leaves provide deep shade. The
foot-long pods contain sweet pulp and edible seeds, thought
to be the "wild honey and locusts" that sustained St. John
in the wilderness. AREAS: J

CINNAMOMUM

C. camphora (camphor tree)
A slow-growing species that has attractive light green
leaves with silvery blue undersides, the camphor tree when
young can be sheared for use in hedges; as it matures to a
height of 50 feet, it takes on a rounded crown that can become very wide spreading. The tree casts deep shade and
has an aggressive root system, making it hard to grow
plants under it. AREAS: E J

CITRUS

Citrus varieties (orange, lemon, grapefruit, pomelo,
tangelo, lime, tangerine)
These low, broad, relatively fast-growing trees provide dec-
oration as well as bountiful eating with their fragrant spring
bloom and colorful fruit. They grow in warmer sections of
the recommended areas and do best in well-drained soil
and sheltered locations. AREAS: E J

CUPANIA See *Cupaniopsis*

CUPANIOPSIS, also called CUPANIA

C. anacardioides (carrotwood, tuckeroo)
This tree, whose leathery green leaves are divided into
six to 10 leaflets, provides good shade and grows to 30
feet tall with a spread of 20 feet. It is resistant to seaside winds and air pollution. AREAS: J

ELM See *Ulmus*

EUCALYPTUS

Decorative and fast growing (some species grow as much as 10 to 15 feet a year when young), eucalyptus trees are noted for their graceful limbs, attractive, peeling bark and striking, usually fragrant, blue-green leaves. Many species bloom in late summer or fall and even through winter. Also called gum trees because of their resinous sap, they thrive in dry soil and resist pests and diseases.

E. camaldulensis, also called E. rostrata
(red gum, river red gum)
The red gum, a popular shade tree, grows 80 to 120 feet tall and has mottled tan-to-gray bark and drooping branches that bear long slim leaves.　　AREAS:⬚⬚⬚⬚⬚⬚⬚⬚J

E. citriodora, also called E. maculata citriodora
(lemon-scented gum)
This species, which grows 50 to 75 feet tall, is delightful near a patio because of the lemonlike scent of its long, pointed, greenish yellow leaves. The high-branching trunk is slim and gracefully straight, the bark a whitish pink or greenish white.　　AREAS:⬚⬚⬚⬚⬚⬚⬚⬚J

E. erythrocorys (red cap gum)
The red cap gum grows 10 to 30 feet tall, with red branches rising above a white trunk that is often divided into multiple stems.　　AREAS:⬚⬚⬚⬚⬚⬚⬚⬚J

E. ficifolia (red flowering gum, scarlet flowering gum)
The showiest of the eucalyptus species, the red-flowering gum grows 20 to 40 feet tall, with a dense, round crown that provides ample shade. It has bronze-red foliage when young, dark reddish brown bark, and masses of brilliant red or pink flowers, which are most abundant in January and February and again from July to October. It tolerates wind and salt air.　　AREAS:⬚⬚⬚⬚⬚⬚⬚⬚J

E. leucoxylon (white ironbark)
The white ironbark grows 40 to 80 feet tall, with hanging, sickle-shaped, gray-green leaves accented by clusters of white flowers from late fall until spring. The slender graceful trunk is covered with smooth white or mottled green bark.　　AREAS:⬚⬚⬚⬚⬚⬚⬚⬚J

E. polyanthemos (red box gum, silver dollar tree, Australian beech)
An upright low-branching tree that grows 30 to 70 feet tall, the red box gum is used as a windbreak in seaside and desert locations, and bears clusters of small white flowers in winter and early spring.　　AREAS:⬚⬚⬚⬚⬚⬚⬚⬚J

E. pulverulenta (silver mountain gum)
The sprawling angular branches of this species, which can grow 15 to 30 feet tall, add interesting patterns and color to a garden landscape; they bear round, bright silvery blue leaves, which clasp the stems. The trees make good windbreaks and screens.　　AREAS:⬚⬚⬚⬚⬚⬚⬚⬚J

E. rudis (desert gum)
A sturdy compact tree that grows 30 to 50 feet tall, the desert gum has pendulous branches, long, slender, bluish green leaves, rough red-brown bark, and clusters of tiny white flowers in late summer and fall. It withstands drought and salt air.　　AREAS:⬚⬚⬚⬚⬚⬚⬚⬚J

E. sideroxylon rosea (red ironbark, pink ironbark)
This tree is named for its large pendulous clusters of pink flowers, which bloom in midwinter and early spring, and

RED FLOWERING GUM, SCARLET FLOWERING GUM
Eucalyptus ficifolia

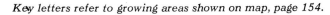

Key letters refer to growing areas shown on map, page 154.

for its rough red-brown bark, which splits to reveal bright red bark. It grows to 30 to 50 feet and is used as a single ornament or street tree. AREAS: J

E. torquata (coral gum, goldfield gum)
A slim, erect tree with several reddish trunks, the coral gum grows 15 to 20 feet tall and is lovely by itself or near a patio. It has supple long branches that seem to weep beneath the weight of its gray-green leaves and masses of coral pink to red flowers, which appear intermittently throughout the year. AREAS: J

FICUS (FIG)
(See also Vines, page 150.)
F. benjamin (weeping fig, Java fig, weeping Chinese banyan, Benjamin fig)
The weeping fig, which only grows in frost-free regions, provides quick shade, reaching a height of 30 to 50 feet in Florida and about half that size in the drier California air. Masses of shiny, dark green, 3- to 6-inch leaves that cloak its drooping branches make it a handsome ornamental tree for patios. Mature trees bear small, round, inedible reddish figs. AREAS: E J

FRAXINUS (ASH)
(See also Deciduous trees, page 104.)
F. uhdei (shamel ash, evergreen ash)
This shade tree, straight and narrow when young, gradually forms a dense round top of glossy, dark green leaves. It grows rapidly—up to 30 feet in 10 years—eventually reaching over 70 feet. AREAS: J

GRAPEFRUIT See *Citrus*

GREVILLEA
G. robusta (silk oak)
Columnar when young, then broadening at the top, silk oaks grow rapidly to about 75 feet. Their fernlike, dark green leaves are silvery beneath and provide ample shade. Branches bear large flat clusters of yellow-orange flowers in early spring. The trees thrive in frost-free parts of the areas recommended and should be planted in dry soil with good drainage. AREAS: E J

GUAVA See *Psidium*
GUM See *Eucalyptus*
HOLLY See Broad-leaved evergreen shrubs *Ilex*
HONG KONG ORCHID TREE See *Bauhinia*
IRONBARK See *Eucalyptus*
LAUREL, CALIFORNIA See *Umbellularia*
LEMON See *Citrus*
LIME See *Citrus*

LITCHI
L. chinensis (lychee, litchi nut)
A round-topped tree that grows slowly to 40 feet tall in frost-free parts of Areas E and J, the lychee provides shade, ornament and edible fruit. Its leathery leaves, reddish when young, turn dark green with age. The bright red fruits that mature in June are delicious to eat fresh, dried or preserved in syrup. AREAS: E J

MAGNOLIA
(See also Deciduous trees, page 106.)
M. grandiflora and varieties (Southern magnolia, bull bay)
This magnificent ornamental and shade tree grows in a pyramidal shape to 90 feet tall and 40 feet or more across; it bears long, lustrous, leathery, dark green leaves and 8- to

SHAMEL ASH, EVERGREEN ASH
Fraxinus uhdei

128

12-inch, heavily scented white flowers, which bloom chiefly in spring and summer although occasional blossoms open throughout the year. It thrives in moist fertile soil and is highly pest resistant.   AREAS: ☐☐ D E ☐☐ I J

M. virginiana, also called *M. glauca* (sweet bay)
The sweet bay has deep green leaves with white undersides and is semievergreen. It grows rapidly to 40 to 60 feet and bears fragrant, round white flowers, 2 to 3 inches across, in late spring.   AREAS: ☐☐ D E ☐☐ I J

MELALEUCA
M. leucadendron, also called *M. quinquenervia*
(cajeput tree, swamp tea tree, punk tree, paper bush)
Decorative by itself or as an accent, this tree provides shade and tolerates wind and seashore conditions. Slim and erect, it grows swiftly to 40 feet tall in frost-free regions and has stiff, silvery green leaves and spongy gray bark. White flower spikes that look like bottlebrushes bloom in summer and fall.   AREAS: ☐☐☐ E ☐☐☐ J

MYRTLE, OREGON See *Umbellularia*
MYRTLE, WILLOW See *Agonis*
OAK See *Quercus*
OAK, SILK See *Grevillea*
OCTOPUS TREE See *Brassaia*

OLEA (OLIVE)
O. europaea (common olive)
The common olive grows slowly to a height of 20 to 30 feet, forming a dense round head of silvery green, willowlike leaves. Its gnarled gray trunk and twisted limbs are a common sight in California and southern Arizona, where the tree is widely used for shade and ornament. Its fruit, which ripens in fall, is a commercial crop in California, but a nuisance in gardens. The ripe olives will stain paving and patio furniture. The trees do best in well-drained soil.   AREAS: ☐☐☐☐☐☐☐ J

ORANGE See *Citrus*
OREGON MYRTLE See *Umbellularia*
PAPER BUSH See *Melaleuca*
PEAR See *Pyrus*
PEPPER TREE See *Schinus*
PEPPERMINT TREE See *Agonis*

PITTOSPORUM
These trees, notable for their decorative foliage and fragrant flowers, are suitable near patios or as individual lawn trees. The species listed below grow slowly, thrive in dry soil and withstand wind and salt air. *(See also Broadleaved evergreen shrubs, page 142.)*

P. phillyraeoides (weeping or willow pittosporum)
The drooping branches of this species, which grows 20 to 25 feet tall, bear narrow, silvery green leaves. Small, fragrant yellow flowers bloom in late winter and early spring, followed by small, inedible orange-yellow berries. The trees need very dry soil.   AREAS: ☐☐☐☐☐☐☐ J

P. rhombifolium (diamond leaf pittosporum,
Queensland pittosporum)
The diamond-shaped, glossy green leaves of this pyramidal 20- to 35-foot tree provide excellent shade; an abundance of tiny, fragrant white flowers appears in spring, followed by large clusters of bright yellow-orange berries in fall and winter. The species is popular as a street tree in southern California.   AREAS: ☐☐☐☐☐☐☐ J

Key letters refer to growing areas shown on map, page 154.

SOUTHERN MAGNOLIA, BULL BAY
Magnolia grandiflora

COMMON OLIVE
Olea europaea

LIVE OAK
Quercus virginiana

EVERGREEN ELM
Ulmus parvifolia pendens

PSIDIUM
P. cattleianum (strawberry guava)
Named for its tasty red fruit, the strawberry guava grows 15 to 25 feet tall with open, spreading branches and a trunk (often multistemmed) notable for its smooth brown bark. Many-stamened, small white flowers set among dark green leaves are followed by 1- to 2-inch berries that ripen in fall and early winter. If trimmed, the trees make good hedges and screens. They should be planted only in relatively frost-free regions. AREAS: E J

PUNK TREE See *Melaleuca*

PYRUS
(See also Deciduous trees, page 109.)
P. kawakami (evergreen pear)
Although its fruit is inconspicuous and inedible, and it is actually semievergreen, the evergreen pear is a handsome ornamental tree in the 20- to 40-foot range. Its drooping branches bear lustrous, bright green leaves; profuse clusters of fragrant white flowers appear in winter and early spring. Fast-growing young trees require staking and pruning to become well shaped. They should be planted only in relatively frost-free areas. AREAS: E J

QUEENSLAND UMBRELLA TREE See *Brassaia*

QUERCUS (OAK)
Most evergreen oaks, like their deciduous relatives *(page 109)*, are noted for their great size, long life and dense, shade-giving foliage. The species recommended below grow to 60 feet tall or more, with an equal or greater spread.

Q. agrifolia (California live oak, coast live oak)
An impressive shade or lawn tree, the California live oak grows rapidly to a height of 35 to 70 feet. Strong coastal winds often contort its massive branches into stunningly bizarre shapes. Its 1- to 3-inch leaves are somewhat holly-like, with spiny edges. AREAS: J

Q. ilex (holly oak, holm oak)
Named for its shiny hollylike leaves, this 40- to 60-foot tree is pest and disease resistant and well suited to seaside gardens. AREAS: J

Q. suber (cork oak)
An interesting ornamental tree, this species has thick rough bark that is the source of commercial cork. As the tree grows to 40 to 60 feet, it assumes a massive, round head of small shimmering leaves with silver-gray undersides. It does best in dry soil. AREAS: D E G J

Q. virginiana (live oak)
Live oaks are magnificent ornaments for large gardens; their immense branches spread to twice the height of the tree, which may reach 50 feet, and bear shiny oval leaves and glistening brown acorns. The trees may drop their foliage in northern regions. AREAS: D E G J

ST. JOHN'S BREAD See *Ceratonia*
SAPODILLA See *Achras*
SCHEFFLERA See *Brassaia*

SCHINUS (PEPPER TREE)
The two species listed make fine shade and ornamental trees; they grow 20 to 40 feet tall with an equal spread and have rounded tops and frondlike leaves. Female trees bear tiny, inedible pink-to-red berries.

S. molle (California pepper tree)
Fast growing and tolerant of almost any soil, the California pepper tree has a gnarled trunk and wide-spreading, gracefully drooping branches that bear tiny, yellowish white flowers in summer.   AREAS: ☐☐☐☐☐☐☐ J ☐

S. terebinthifolius (Brazilian pepper tree)
The branches of this species are more upright than those of the California pepper tree, the leaves heavier and less feathery.   AREAS: ☐☐ E ☐☐ J ☐

SILK OAK See *Grevillea*
SILVER DOLLAR TREE See *Eucalyptus*
STERCULIA DIVERSIFOLIA See *Brachychiton*
SWAMP TEA TREE See *Melaleuca*
SWEET BAY See *Magnolia*
TUCKEROO See *Cupaniopsis*

ULMUS (ELM)
(See also Deciduous trees, page 112.)
U. parvifolia pendens, also called *U. parvifolia sempervirens* (Chinese evergreen elm)
A good patio and screening tree, the wide-spreading Chinese evergreen elm provides quick shade, growing rapidly to 40 to 50 feet tall. Its arching branches bear small, leathery, dark green leaves.   AREAS: ☐☐☐ E ☐☐ J ☐

UMBELLULARIA
U. californica (California laurel, California bay, Oregon myrtle)
This delightful patio or street tree grows 20 to 50 feet tall and bears leathery yellow-green leaves that have a camphorlike fragrance and provide dense shade. Clusters of small, yellowish green flowers bloom in spring, followed by yellowish green, inedible fruit.   AREAS: ☐☐☐☐☐☐ I J ☐

WATTLE See *Acacia*
WEEPING CHINESE BANYAN See *Ficus*
WILLOW MYRTLE See *Agonis*

Evergreen shrubs

For purposes of classification, the horticultural line between a tree and a shrub is drawn at 20 feet; nature, however, uses no such ruler; some trees on pages 120-131, such as the bottlebrush, make equally fine shrubs; some shrubs can be used as trees. Much depends on the environment, and on how the plant is pruned and fed. At the other end of the scale, many low-growing shrubs can be used as high ground covers *(pages 146-148)*. Evergreen shrubs, like evergreen trees, are subdivided into narrow-leaved and broad-leaved groups. Fast-growing shrubs add 2 to 3 feet a year; slow-growing ones add less than a foot.

Narrow-leaved evergreen shrubs

ARBORVITAE See *Thuja*
CEDAR, RED See *Juniperus*

CHAMAECYPARIS (FALSE CYPRESS)
False cypresses come in many shapes and sizes. Although most species ultimately mature to full trees *(page 121)*, many, like the varieties listed below, are essentially shrubs in gardens. All need moist growing conditions and shelter from wind, and respond to light shaping with hedge shears.

C. obtusa and varieties (Hinoki false cypress)
Hinoki false cypresses have lacy sprays of branchlets

SLENDER HINOKI FALSE CYPRESS
Chamaecyparis obtusa gracilis

Key letters refer to growing areas shown on map, page 154.

sheathed in lustrous blackish green leaves. Slow-growing varieties are valued as accent plants and in rock gardens. One of the most elegant types is the slender *C. obtusa gracilis,* which rarely exceeds 6 feet in height and bears lustrous dark green foliage.   AREAS: B C | | | | I J

C. pisifera and varieties (Sawara false cypress)
This species includes many handsome, easily grown varieties. The thread false cypress, *C. pisifera filifera,* named for its long drooping branches wrapped in tightly furled dark green foliage, grows slowly in a wide pyramidal shape. Moss Sawara false cypress *(C. pisifera squarrosa)* is a well-branched, pyramidal shrub noted for its soft blue, mossy needles.   AREAS: B C | | | | I J

CYPRESS, FALSE See *Chamaecyparis*

JUNIPERUS (JUNIPER)
Junipers, hardy plants that need little care, thrive in sunshine in almost any well-drained soil and tolerate dry rocky locations. *(See also Ground covers, page 147.)*

J. chinensis and varieties (Chinese juniper)
The wide-spreading, gray-green Pfitzer variety grows 3 to 4 feet high and is one of the few junipers that can stand light shade; it is an excellent choice for planting next to the house, although it does require frequent pruning. A dense, blue-green pyramidal variety, *J. chinensis pyramidalis,* retains its formal shape with little or no pruning. The Hollywood juniper *(J. chinensis torulosa)* is a dense, rich green pyramidal shrub that has curiously twisted branchlets.   AREAS: B C D E F G H I J

J. communis and varieties (common juniper)
One of the hardiest and most popular varieties is the prostrate juniper *(J. communis depressa),* a dense, spreading shrub. It rarely grows more than 3 to 4 feet tall and is often used in plantings near houses and for covering rocky slopes. The outsides of its flat green needles turn bronze in fall, contrasting with their blue-white inner surfaces. The slim columnar shapes of dark green Irish *(J. communis stricta)* and blue-green Swedish *(J. communis suecica)* varieties make dramatic accents.   AREAS: A B C D E F G H I J

J. conferta (shore juniper)
A favorite among seaside gardeners, the shore juniper forms a green carpet, seldom over a foot tall, that requires only occasional pruning.   AREAS: C D E G I J

J. procumbens and varieties (Japanese garden juniper)
Wide-spreading branches and stiff, upright twigs covered with blue-green needles make this species a fine choice as a ground cover and for use in plantings around modern homes, as it seldom grows taller than 2 feet. A dwarf variety, *J. procumbens nana,* only a few inches tall, is delightful in rock gardens.   AREAS: C D E G I J

J. sabina and varieties (savin juniper)
Savin junipers are wide vase-shaped plants 6 to 8 feet tall with arching branch tips and thick foliage. They tolerate alkaline soil and urban smog.

AREAS: B C D E F G H I J

J. scopulorum and varieties
(Rocky Mountain juniper, western red cedar)
Most varieties of Rocky Mountain junipers are narrowly pyramidal in shape and have blue-green foliage that often takes on purple, gray or silvery blue tints in cold weather. The varieties called 'Gray Gleam' and 'Pathfinder' are ex-

HOLLYWOOD JUNIPER
Juniperus chinensis torulosa

CANAERT RED CEDAR
Juniperus virginiana canaertii

cellent accent plants standing alone and also make fine, easily sheared hedges. 'Table Top Blue' is a semispreading flat-topped variety and 'Lakewood Globe' is a blue-green spherical shrub. AREAS: | | |C|D| |F|G|H|I|J|

J. virginiana and varieties (eastern red cedar)
Most eastern red cedars are pyramidal or columnar in habit, requiring little shearing to maintain thick foliage. They grow in nearly any soil and make fine hedges or individual specimens. Canaert red cedar *(J. virginiana canaertii)* is pyramidal with rich, dark green foliage that is borne in tufts and retains its color in winter, unlike most eastern red cedars, which turn bronze or brownish. The gray-green foliage of Dundee juniper *(J. virginiana pyramidiformis hillii)* turns plum-purple, providing a colorful note in winter gardens. AREAS: |A|B|C|D|E| |G| |I|J|

PINUS (PINE)
Besides the familiar tall-growing species *(page 123),* pines include forms that, with proper trimming, make excellent garden shrubs. They do best in light soil and, once established, can stand considerable dryness.

P. aristata (bristlecone pine, hickory pine)
Bristlecone pines have a picturesque bushlike growth, often with several trunks, and bear clusters of short blue-green needles. Growth is so slow that 20-year-old plants are only 5 to 8 feet tall. AREAS: |A|B|C| | |F| |H|I|J|

P. cembra (Swiss stone pine)
Swiss stone pines are among the most aristocratic landscaping materials. They are very slow growing and seldom reach higher than 25 feet. They keep their neat conical shape, densely covered with fat pompons of stiff blue-green needles, without pruning. AREAS: |A|B|C| | | | |H|I| |

P. mugo mugo, also called *P. montana*
(mugo pine, Swiss mountain pine)
One of the few naturally low-growing pines—it rarely reaches 8 feet, and often only half that height—the mugo pine has long been a favorite for low plantings in home landscapes. Its spreading branches are thickly set with stiff, bright green needles. AREAS: |A|B|C| | |F| |H|I| |

RED CEDAR See *Juniperus*

TAXUS (YEW)
Extremely slow growing for their first five years, the yews thrive on shearing, forming handsome dense hedges, and can be sculptured into fanciful shapes in formal gardens. They tolerate full sun to nearly full shade, but need fertile well-drained soil.

T. baccata and varieties (English yew)
Among the most popular shrub varieties available are the shortleaf English yew *(T. baccata adpressa),* a dense spreading shrub, and the Irish yew *(T. baccata stricta),* a narrow columnar shrub. AREAS: | | |C|D| | | | |I|J|

T. cuspidata and varieties (Japanese yew)
One of the best ornamental varieties is the upright Japanese yew *(T. cuspidata capitata),* which has deep green foliage and a broadly pyramidal form that makes it an excellent choice for tall hedges. AREAS: | |B|C|D| |F| | |I| |

T. media and varieties (intermediate yew)
Intermediate yews are hardy evergreens that generally need little or no pruning. Slow-growing favorites include

Key letters refer to growing areas shown on map, page 154.

MUGO PINE, SWISS MOUNTAIN PINE
Pinus mugo mugo

UPRIGHT JAPANESE YEW
Taxus cuspidata capitata

HICKS YEW
Taxus media hicksii

Brown's yew *(T. media brownii),* a globular variety, and Hatfield's yew *(T. media hatfieldii),* a broadly conical, dark green shrub. One of the narrowest varieties is Hicks yew *(T. media hicksii),* a dense, flat-topped columnar bush. Topped and trimmed, it is one of the best yews for low hedges.   AREAS: ☐ B C D ☐ F ☐ ☐ I ☐

THUJA, also called THUYA (ARBORVITAE)
Essentially broad, pyramidal trees, arborvitae also include dwarf and shrubby varieties; some make excellent hedge plants, as they react well to pruning. They do best in rich moist soil and full sun, but can stand fairly heavy shade.

T. occidentalis and varieties (American arborvitae)
The dark green foliage of these arborvitae is scalelike and arranged in flat lacy branchlets. The Douglas arborvitae *(T. occidentalis douglasii pyramidalis)* is a graceful conical shrub that grows slowly to 18 to 20 feet, with feathery, twisted foliage.   AREAS: A B C ☐ ☐ F G H I ☐

T. orientalis and varieties (Oriental arborvitae)
The foliage of these arborvitae is similar to that of the American species *(above),* but is often a lighter shade of green. Two desirable low-growing varieties are the bright green Siebold arborvitae *(T. orientalis sieboldii),* a dense rounded bush, and Berkman's golden arborvitae *(T. orientalis aurea nana),* a tight oval plant with foliage that changes from gold in spring to yellow green in summer to bronze gold in winter.   AREAS: ☐ ☐ D E ☐ G ☐ I J

YEW See *Taxus*

Broad-leaved evergreen shrubs

ABELIA
A. grandiflora (glossy abelia)
A moundlike shrub that grows 3 to 5 feet high, glossy abelia has small, shiny, bronze-green leaves that are evergreen except in Area C, and small trumpet-shaped pink flowers from spring until frost. Glossy abelia does best in full sun and well-drained soil.   AREAS: ☐ ☐ C D E ☐ G ☐ I J

ANDROMEDA See *Pieris*
ARALIA See *Fatsia*

AUCUBA
A. japonica (Japanese aucuba)
Japanese aucuba is a handsome 6- to 15-foot shrub for planting in partial shade. Female plants bear red berries among glossy 4- to 7-inch leaves in fall and winter, provided there is a male plant close by. The variety *A. japonica variegata* is called the gold-dust tree because of its mottled yellow foliage. Aucubas do best in rich soil and tolerate drought and city conditions.   AREAS: ☐ ☐ D E ☐ G ☐ I J

AZALEA See *Rhododendron*

BERBERIS (BARBERRY)
Armed with spiny-edged glossy leaves and thorns, barberries make formidable hedges and corner plants where shortcuts might otherwise be tempting. The graceful arching branches of most varieties bear a profusion of bright yellow flowers in early spring, augmented in fall by black or red berries. Barberries grow best in full sun and moist well-drained soil. *(See also Deciduous shrubs, page 113.)*

B. julianae (wintergreen barberry)
This dense vigorous shrub is the most popular of the evergreen barberries. Its upright branches, amply lined with 2-

DOUGLAS ARBORVITAE
Thuja occidentalis douglasii pyramidalis

GOLD-DUST TREE
Aucuba japonica variegata

to 3-inch gleaming dark green leaves, form a 3- to 5-foot mound; plants bear golden yellow blossoms in spring, followed by blue-black berries.   AREAS: | | |C|D| |G| |I|J|

B. mentorensis (Mentor barberry)
The semievergreen Mentor barberry grows upright to 5 to 7 feet and bears yellow flowers, followed by dark red berries. In northern parts of Area C its leaves turn shades of yellow and red before falling in very late autumn. Plants thrive in dry or moist soil.   AREAS: | | |C|D| |G| |I|J|

BLUEBERRY See *Vaccinium*
BOTTLEBRUSH See *Callistemon*
BOX See *Buxus*
BOX, FALSE See *Pachistima*
BOXWOOD See *Buxus*
BOXWOOD, MOUNTAIN See *Pachistima*
BOXWOOD, OREGON See *Pachistima*

BRUNFELSIA
B. calycina floribunda (yesterday, today and tomorrow)
This shrub grows about 3 feet high with an equal spread and bears small, round, white-centered purple flowers that fade to lavender the second day and to nearly white the third day, hence the common name. Bushes bloom almost constantly in frost-free areas, with the greatest flowering in springtime, and grow best in partial shade and moist acid soil. The species is recommended only for the warmest parts of Area E.   AREAS: | | | |E| | | |J|

BUXUS (BOXWOOD, BOX)
A favorite for edging rose beds and garden walks, boxwood is also used for formal hedges and ornamental shapes because it responds well to shearing. Untrimmed, the soft billows of fragrant foliage make lovely informal hedges. Boxwood grows slowly, needs moist soil and does especially well under the high shade of deciduous trees.

B. microphylla japonica (Japanese little-leaved boxwood)
B. microphylla koreana (Korean little-leaved boxwood)
Japanese little-leaved boxwood grows 4 feet tall; the Korean variety grows half that height. Both have glossy green leaves that turn yellowish or tan in winter. Their growth is more open than that of common boxwood *(below)*.
   B. microphylla japonica AREAS: | | | |D| |G| |I|J|
   B. microphylla koreana AREAS: | | |C|D| |G| |I|J|

B. sempervirens (common boxwood)
Common boxwood's lustrous blue-green foliage can be sheared to form hedges 2 to 6 feet high; unpruned, it may grow 10 or more feet tall.   AREAS: | | | |D|E| |G| |I|J|

CALIFORNIA LILAC See *Ceanothus*

CALLISTEMON (BOTTLEBRUSH)
C. citrinus, also called **C. lanceolatus** (lemon bottlebrush)
A fast-growing shrub with pendulous branches, the lemon bottlebrush is useful as an ornamental and screening plant that usually grows 6 to 10 feet tall. Its many-stamened red flowers, which resemble bottlebrushes, bloom from midwinter until midsummer amidst narrow gray-green leaves that are a coppery hue when young. Plants grow best in dry soil and full sun.   AREAS: | | | |E| | | |J|

CAMELLIA
C. japonica and varieties (common camellia)
The common camellia is best known for its lovely flowers, 2 to 5 inches across, which bloom from fall to spring in

LEMON BOTTLEBRUSH
Callistemon citrinus

COMMON CAMELLIA
Camellia japonica

Key letters refer to growing areas shown on map, page 154.

warmer areas and in early spring in cooler areas. The flowers range from single to double and from white to pink to red, depending on the variety. Plants, which grow 6 to 10 feet tall, have lustrous leaves and can be used as single ornaments or in hedges or screens. They thrive under almost all light conditions provided the soil is acid and rich in organic matter. AREAS: | | |D|E| | |I|J|

C. sasanqua (sasanqua camellia)
Smaller than the common camellia, usually growing 5 to 6 feet tall, the sasanqua makes a lovely hedge plant. It bears 3-inch white or pink, single or semidouble blooms from fall through early winter. AREAS: | | |D|E| | |I|J|

CAPE JASMINE See *Gardenia*

CARISSA
C. macrocarpa, also called *C. grandiflora,* and varieties (Natal plum)
This fast-growing thorny shrub with oval, dark green leaves produces small, fragrant white flowers and edible plum-shaped fruits that taste like cranberries. Upright types grow 5 to 8 feet tall and are suitable for hedges, while some low-growing varieties never grow more than 2 feet high and make good ground covers. Plants need sun but grow in most soils. The species is recommended only for warmer regions. AREAS: | | |E| | | |J|

CEANOTHUS
Ceanothus species and hybrids
(ceanothus, California lilac, wild lilac)
The ceanothus' clusters of blue, lavender or white flowers make a magnificent display in early spring. Plants vary from low-lying shrubs to upright types 6 to 18 feet tall, thrive in seaside locations, are highly tolerant of drought, and require well-drained soil. AREAS: | | | | | |I|J|

CHERRY LAUREL See *Prunus*
CHINESE SACRED BAMBOO See *Nandina*

COCCOLOBA, also called COCCOLOBIS
C. uvifera (sea grape, shore grape)
A densely branching decorative and screening shrub that can grow 20 to 25 feet tall, the sea grape thrives in seaside locations. It bears foot-long clusters of tiny ivory-white flowers in early spring among coarse, red-veined, nearly circular leaves up to 8 inches across. The small, purple, grapelike fruits that hang in bunches in summer and fall make a tasty jelly. Sea grape is recommended only for the warmer parts of Areas E and J. AREAS: | | |E| | | |J|

CODIAEUM
C. variegatum and varieties (croton)
Crotons range from 3 to 10 feet in height and offer great diversity in leaf shape and color. Leaves are often multicolored, flamboyantly combining yellow, orange, pink, red and crimson with shades of green. Crotons make attractive plantings near houses and may be used as screens or hedges. They will grow in most moist, well-drained soils in full sun or light shade but are recommended only for frost-free parts of Areas E and J. AREAS: | | |E| | | |J|

COTONEASTER
(See also Deciduous shrubs, page 114.)
C. dammeri, also called *C. humifusa*
(bearberry cotoneaster)
This trailing shrub bears small white flowers in early summer and red berries in fall. It makes a fine ground cover

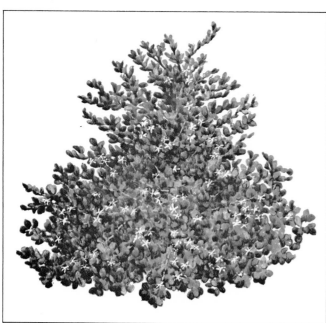

NATAL PLUM
Carissa macrocarpa

CROTON
Codiaeum variegatum

(it grows only about a foot tall) and a decorative planting
for rock gardens.   AREAS: | |C|D|E| |G| |I|J|

C. horizontalis (rock spray, rock cotoneaster)
A wide-spreading plant, rock spray grows up to 3 feet high.
In early summer it bears pinkish white flowers; bright red
berries appear in fall, when the semievergreen, shiny green
foliage turns a reddish color. Rock spray is excellent for
ground covers or rock gardens or in the foreground of shrub
plantings.   AREAS: | |C|D|E| |G| |I|J|

C. parneyi, also called *C. lactea* (Parney's red clusterberry)
This species grows 5 to 8 feet tall; it bears tiny white flowers in spring and clusters of red berries in winter among
leathery, dark green leaves. It is good for screens and may
be trimmed to make hedges.   AREAS: | | |D|E| | |I|J|

CROTON See *Codiaeum*
DAHOON See *Ilex*

DAPHNE
(See also Deciduous shrubs, page 115.)
D. cneorum (rose daphne, garland flower)
This slow-growing shrub rarely reaches 1 foot high; its narrow 1-inch leaves form a dense mat. Bright, fragrant, rosy
pink flowers appear in small clusters at the branch tips in
spring and occasionally in fall. It is excellent for rock gardens. Plants grow best in cool, moist, nonacid soil in sun or
light shade and should be protected with marsh hay in
cold northern winters.   AREAS: | |C|D| | | |I| |

ELAEAGNUS
*(See also Deciduous trees, page 104, and Deciduous shrubs,
page 115.)*
E. pungens and varieties (thorny elaeagnus, silverberry)
This plant thrives in almost any soil in sun or light shade,
grows 6 to 15 feet tall unless pruned and makes a useful
screen or prickly hedge. In fall it bears small, hanging silvery white blossoms that are fragrant, followed by brown
berries that turn red. Some varieties have foliage with yel-
low or creamy white markings.   AREAS: | | | |E| |G| |J|

VARIEGATED THORNY ELAEAGNUS
Elaeagnus pungens variegata

ENGLISH LAUREL See *Prunus*

ERICA (HEATH)
E. herbacea, also called *E. carnea,* and varieties
(spring heath)
A low-growing plant that seldom exceeds 1 foot in height,
spring heath has needlelike foliage; small spikes of tiny
pink, crimson or white blossoms appear in winter and
spring. Plants can be used in the foreground of shrub plant-
ings or as ground covers.   AREAS: | |C|D| | | |I|J|

E. mediterranea (Mediterranean heath, biscay heath)
This shrub grows 5 to 7 feet tall, with lilac-pink flowers
that bloom in early spring.   AREAS: | | |D| | | |I| |

LOQUAT, JAPANESE PLUM
Eriobotrya japonica

ERIOBOTRYA
E. japonica (loquat, Japanese plum)
Loquat is a 10- to 25-foot-tall shrub that has massive (6- to
12-inch) dark green leaves, rusty brown on their undersides. From late summer through fall it bears clusters of
small fragrant white flowers; in spring it produces small,
tart yellow-to-orange fruit that can be eaten raw or made
into jams, jellies and pies. It is excellent for screening;
trained to a single stem it makes an exotic small tree. It is
very sturdy and grows best in moist well-drained soil and
full sun or partial shade.   AREAS: | | | |E| | | |J|

Key letters refer to growing areas shown on map, page 154.

JAPANESE FATSIA
Fatsia japonica

GARDENIA, CAPE JASMINE
Gardenia jasminoides

ENGLISH HOLLY
Ilex aquifolium

EUONYMUS
(See also Deciduous shrubs, page 115, Ground covers, page 146, and Vines, page 150.)
E. fortunei and varieties (winter creeper)
Winter creepers are among the hardiest of broad-leaved evergreens. One variety, bigleaf winter creeper (*E. fortunei vegetus*), can be trained as a wall or chimney climber, but if left to itself it will make a 4-foot shrub, often spreading to twice that in diameter. Most large-growing types have 1- to 2-inch roundish leaves and in fall bear tiny pink capsules that open to expose fleshy orange fruit. Varieties known as Emerald Hybrids vary in form from 'Emerald Cushion,' which grows 1½ to 2 feet high with a spread of 3 feet, to 'Emerald Beauty,' 5 to 6 feet tall and spreading 8 to 10 feet. AREAS: B C D E G I J

E. japonicus and varieties (evergreen euonymus)
This species may grow 10 to 15 feet tall, but it is more attractive if pruned smaller; it makes a fine hedge, screen or individual plant with lustrous, bright green leaves 1 to 3 inches long. Inconspicuous greenish white flowers in summer are followed by tiny, pinkish orange capsules, which open to display orange fruit. Some varieties have leaves with white or yellow markings. AREAS: D E G I J

EUPHORBIA
E. pulcherrima (poinsettia)
A rangy shrub that grows rapidly to a height of 4 to 10 feet, the poinsettia has long, gleaming green leaves and in fall and winter bears the large (8 to 12 inches across) red, white or pink flowers that are associated with Christmas. Plants should be grown outdoors only in frost-free parts of the recommended areas. AREAS: E J

FALSE BOX See *Pachistima*

FATSIA
F. japonica, also called *Aralia japonica, A. sieboldii* (Japanese fatsia)
This ornamental species grows 4 to 8 feet tall with glossy fan-shaped leaves, up to a foot across; in fall and winter, upright clusters of small white flowers appear, followed by small, inedible blue berries. Plants grow in nearly any soil in sun or light shade but are recommended only for frost-free regions. AREAS: E J

FATSIA PAPYRIFERA See *Tetrapanax*

FEIJOA
F. sellowiana (pineapple guava)
A bushy many-branched shrub 6 to 8 feet tall, the pineapple guava can reach 18 to 20 feet unless pruned. It is grown for its 3-inch gray-green leaves, chalky white underneath, and its pineapple-flavored, 3-inch reddish green fruit, which appears in fall after a summer blossoming of red-stamened white flowers. It can be planted alone or in hedges or screens. AREAS: E J

FIRE THORN See *Pyracantha*
FLAME-OF-THE-WOODS See *Ixora*

GARDENIA
G. jasminoides and varieties (gardenia, cape jasmine)
Gardenias, which usually grow 3 to 5 feet high, are prized for their thick glossy foliage and sweetly scented white flowers, 2 to 3 inches across, which bloom from spring until fall. *G. jasminoides radicans* grows 6 to 12 inches tall. Gardenias may be planted alone or in informal hedges.

They thrive in full sun or partial shade but need rich soil and plenty of moisture.　　　AREAS:☐☐☐E☐☐☐J

GARLAND FLOWER　See *Daphne*
GRAPE, OREGON HOLLY　See *Mahonia*
GRAPE, SEA　See *Coccoloba*
GRAPE, SHORE　See *Coccoloba*
GUAVA, PINEAPPLE　See *Feijoa*
HEATH　See *Erica*

HIBISCUS
(See also Deciduous shrubs, page 116.)
H. rosa-sinensis and varieties
(Chinese hibiscus, rose of China)
The Chinese hibiscus is noted for its dense, glossy foliage and handsome 5- to 8-inch flowers, which are white, pink, red, yellow or orange, depending on the variety. Although each flower lasts only a day, the plants blossom throughout the year. Chinese hibiscus grows 4 to 8 feet high, occasionally higher, and makes an excellent hedge, screen or ornamental plant.　　AREAS:☐☐☐E☐☐☐J

HOLLY　See *Ilex*
HONEYSUCKLE　See *Lonicera*
HUCKLEBERRY　See *Vaccinium*

ILEX (HOLLY)
The distinctive features of hollies are their berries, usually red, and their foliage, a deep, rich green, often edged with spines. Only female plants have berries and usually need at least one male plant nearby to produce them.

I. altaclarensis wilsonii (Wilson holly)
This stunning species bears bright red berries against lustrous thick leaves. It is adaptable to sun or shade and tolerates wind.　　AREAS:☐☐C☐D☐E☐☐G☐☐I☐J

I. aquifolium and varieties (English holly)
English holly, whose branches are often sold for decorations at Christmas, eventually becomes a tree, but it is considered a shrub because it is quite slow growing. Most varieties have stiff glossy leaves 1½ to 2½ inches across, with lobed spiny edges, and pea-sized red or yellow berries. English holly is recommended only for the coastal section of Area J.　　AREAS:☐☐C☐D☐E☐☐☐I☐J

I. cassine (dahoon, dahoon holly)
Dahoon holly, which thrives in wet soil, reaches 20 to 35 feet in height and bears profuse groups of red berries in fall and winter.　　AREAS:☐☐☐D☐E☐☐☐I☐J

I. cornuta and varieties (Chinese holly)
Chinese hollies grow 6 to 10 feet high and have lustrous, dark green leaves 1½ to 5 inches long, and red, orange-red or yellow berries, depending on the variety. Burford holly (*I. cornuta burfordii*), a variety with a rounded form and sparsely spined leaves, bears red berries, sometimes without pollination.　　AREAS:☐☐C☐D☐E☐☐G☐☐I☐J

I. crenata and varieties (Japanese holly)
Japanese hollies range in height from 8 inches to 10 feet or more if unpruned; all have smooth, shiny, spineless leaves and small black berries.　　AREAS:☐☐C☐D☐E☐☐☐I☐J

I. opaca and varieties (American holly)
Slow growing, strong and upright, American hollies occasionally reach 40 feet or more after many years. They are thickly branched, have dense foliage and bear red or yel-

BURFORD HOLLY
Ilex cornuta burfordii

AMERICAN HOLLY
Ilex opaca

Key letters refer to growing areas shown on map, page 154.

MOUNTAIN LAUREL
Kalmia latifolia

OREGON HOLLY GRAPE
Mahonia aquifolium

NANDINA, SACRED BAMBOO
Nandina domestica

low berries. The plants make fine specimens or screen plantings. AREAS: [ ][ ][C][D][E][ ][ ][I][J]

I. vomitoria (yaupon)
Yaupon grows 8 to 20 feet tall unless pruned; it bears small leaves and a profusion of small red berries. Because it responds well to shearing, yaupon makes an excellent hedge. AREAS: [ ][ ][ ][D][E][ ][G][ ][I][J]

IXORA

I. coccinea (flame-of-the-woods, jungle geranium, ixora)
Ixora is a spectacular shrub that grows to 15 feet tall in a compact shape, with glossy, dark green leaves; its red and yellow flowers, about 1 inch across, are borne in clusters through most of the year. Ixoras can be planted singly or used in hedges or screens. They require full sunshine and a well-drained acid soil. The species is recommended only for the warmer parts of Area E. AREAS: [ ][ ][ ][E][ ][ ][ ][ ][ ]

JAPANESE PLUM See *Eriobotrya*

JASMINUM (JASMINE)

(*See also Vines, page 151.*)
J. humile revolutum (Italian jasmine)
This fast-growing shrub reaches 6 to 10 feet; it makes a good decorative plant, hedge or screen with bright green, leathery leaves and small clusters of fragrant 1-inch yellow flowers in summer and fall. AREAS: [ ][ ][ ][D][E][ ][ ][ ][J]

JASMINE, CAPE See *Gardenia*
JUNGLE GERANIUM See *Ixora*

KALMIA

K. latifolia (mountain laurel)
Mountain laurel brightens gardens with large clusters of pink and white flowers in late spring and early summer. It grows 4 to 10 feet tall, requires acid soil and makes a fine screen, hedge or accent shrub. AREAS: [ ][ ][C][D][ ][ ][ ][I][ ]

LAUREL, CHERRY See *Prunus*
LAUREL, ENGLISH See *Prunus*
LAUREL, MOUNTAIN See *Kalmia*
LAUREL, PORTUGAL See *Prunus*
LAURESTINUS See *Viburnum*

LEPTOSPERMUM

L. scoparium hybrids (tea tree)
These drought-resistant shrubs, which vary from 2 to 10 feet in height, are covered in early spring or summer with masses of small pink, crimson, maroon or white flowers, depending on the variety. They are attractive in borders and need very well-drained soil. AREAS: [ ][ ][ ][ ][ ][ ][ ][ ][J]

LEUCOTHOË

L. fontanesiana, also called *L. catesbaei*
(drooping leucothoë)
Drooping leucothoë, which grows about 3 feet high, has arching branches that bear grapelike clusters of waxy white flowers in late spring, and long, dark, shiny leaves that turn bronze in autumn. It is widely used in evergreen plantings with rhododendrons since it does best in moist, acid soil and light shade. AREAS: [ ][ ][C][D][ ][ ][ ][I][J]

LIGUSTRUM (PRIVET)

(*See also Deciduous shrubs, page 116.*)
L. japonicum, and varieties (Japanese privet)
This fast-growing species may reach 15 to 18 feet in height and bears clusters of small white flowers in summer and

black berries in fall. Its lustrous leaves are oval and about 4 inches long. A variety, *L. japonicum texanum*, called waxleafed or lusterleaf ligustrum, grows 6 to 9 feet tall and has larger, thicker leaves; it is popular for low hedges and planting near houses.   AREAS: | | | |DE| G | I |J |

LILAC, CALIFORNIA See *Ceanothus*
LILAC, WILD See *Ceanothus*

LONICERA (HONEYSUCKLE)
(See also Deciduous shrubs, page 117, and Vines, page 151.)
L. nitida (box honeysuckle)
The box honeysuckle, fast growing to 6 feet and bearing 1- to 2-inch, glossy, dark green leaves, makes an excellent screen or hedge, and is commonly so used throughout the South and West. Its flowers, which bloom in late spring and early summer, are creamy white and fragrant. Berries, which are bluish purple, appear in fall. This species will grow in almost any soil and will tolerate light shade as well as seaside conditions.   AREAS: | | | |E| | |I |J |

LOQUAT See *Eriobotrya*

MAHONIA
(See also Ground covers, page 147.)
M. aquifolium (Oregon holly grape)
Oregon holly grape, a lustrous-leaved shrub that grows 2 to 3 feet tall, is used as a border plant, in plantings next to a house and as a tall ground cover. In spring it bears bright yellow flowers; in summer, bluish black, edible, grapelike fruits appear.   AREAS: | | |C|D| G | I |J |

MOUNTAIN BOXWOOD See *Pachistima*
MOUNTAIN LAUREL See *Kalmia*
MYROXYLON See *Xylosma*

MYRTUS
M. communis and varieties (myrtle)
Myrtle grows from 15 inches to 10 feet high depending on the variety, and bears small creamy white flowers in summer and blue-black berries in fall. Both the blossoms and the glossy, bright green, pointed leaves are fragrant. Myrtle makes a fine hedge and responds well to shearing. It needs well-drained soil and full sun to do its best, but also grows in partial shade.   AREAS: | | | |E| G | I |J |

NANDINA
N. domestica (nandina, sacred bamboo)
Nandina, which normally grows 3 to 4 feet high but may reach 8 feet, is a spectacular ornamental shrub that bears large clusters of white flowers in midsummer and bright red berries from fall through much of the winter. It is even more valued for its foliage, which is pink to bronze when the leaves are new in spring, then dark green, and finally bright red to scarlet in fall.   AREAS: | | | |DE| G | I |J |

NATAL PLUM See *Carissa*

NERIUM
N. oleander and varieties (oleander)
A fast-growing plant that may reach 12 feet or more, oleander bears single or double flowers that are white, yellow, pink or red, depending on the variety, and bloom from spring throughout the summer. Its long, leathery, dark green leaves are poisonous. Oleanders need little care, withstand heat and dryness and serve equally well as ornamental shrubs or screens.   AREAS: | | | |DE| G | |J |

Key letters refer to growing areas shown on map, page 154.

OLEANDER
Nerium oleander

JAPANESE ANDROMEDA
Pieris japonica

JAPANESE PITTOSPORUM
Pittosporum tobira

CAROLINA CHERRY LAUREL
Prunus caroliniana

OLEANDER See *Nerium*
OLEANDER, YELLOW See *Thevetia*
OREGON BOXWOOD See *Pachistima*
OREGON HOLLY GRAPE See *Mahonia*

OSMANTHUS
O. heterophyllus, also called *O. ilicifolius* and varieties (holly osmanthus)
A handsome shrub with black-green hollylike leaves, this species ranges from 5 to 15 feet or more in height. Low-growing types are suited to hedges, while tall ones make fine individual plants and screens. All bear inconspicuous, fragrant, greenish yellow flowers followed by small blue-black berries and grow well in moist well-drained soil in full sun or partial shade.   AREAS: ☐☐ D E ☐ G ☐ I J

PACHISTIMA, also called PAXISTIMA
(See also Ground covers, page 147.)
P. myrsinites (myrtle pachistima, mountain boxwood, Oregon boxwood, false box)
A spreading shrub that grows 2 to 4 feet high, myrtle pachistima can be used as a border shrub or a ground cover in the shade. From spring through midsummer it bears tiny reddish flowers that are sometimes followed by tiny inedible white fruit.   AREAS: ☐☐☐☐☐☐☐ I ☐

PARNEY'S RED CLUSTERBERRY See *Cotoneaster*

PHOTINIA
P. serrulata (Chinese photinia)
A fast-growing and handsome shrub, usually 12 to 15 feet high, Chinese photinia makes a splendid decorative plant, hedge or screen. It has 6-inch clusters of small white flowers in spring and bright red berries that ripen in fall and early winter; its best feature, however, is its foliage, which is dark green and lustrous, reaches 8 inches in length, and when forming new leaves is a glorious reddish bronze. Plants do best in a well-drained loam, and will grow in sun or light shade.   AREAS: ☐☐ D E ☐ G ☐ I J

PIERIS (ANDROMEDA)
P. floribunda (mountain andromeda)
Growing 2 to 6 feet tall, this species is one of the most useful evergreen shrubs because of its compact growth, year-round attractiveness and freedom from pests and diseases. Flower buds adorn the plants through winter, blooming in white pyramidal clusters in midspring. The shrub grows in most soils in sun or shade.   AREAS: ☐ B C D ☐☐☐ I ☐

P. japonica (Japanese andromeda)
Japanese andromeda—usually 4 to 5 feet tall—can be planted alone or as a beautiful hedge. In spring, long pendulous clusters of creamy white flowers, reminiscent of lily of the valley, adorn the ends of the stems. The foliage, which is a rich bronze at first, turns dark green as it matures. Plants grow in partial shade, but full sun produces more abundant flowers.   AREAS: ☐☐ C D ☐☐☐ I ☐

PINEAPPLE GUAVA See *Feijoa*

PITTOSPORUM
(See also Broad-leaved evergreen trees, page 129.)
P. tobira (Japanese pittosporum)
A popular shrub for use as a screen or for planting near the house, this dense mound-shaped species usually grows 6 to 12 feet tall and has leathery dark green 2- to 4-inch leaves. Creamy white flowers with a scent similar to orange blossoms bloom in spring and are followed by in-

conspicuous, hard, brown fruit. The plant thrives in most soils in sun or light shade.　AREAS: ☐☐ E ☐ G ☐ J

PLEROMA See *Tibouchina*
PLUM, JAPANESE See *Eriobotrya*
PLUM, NATAL See *Carissa*
POINSETTIA See *Euphorbia*
PORTUGAL LAUREL See *Prunus*
PRINCESS FLOWER See *Tibouchina*
PRIVET See *Ligustrum*

PRUNUS
(See also Deciduous trees, page 109, and Deciduous shrubs, page 117.)
P. caroliniana (Carolina cherry laurel)
This shrub grows rapidly to 20 feet or more and bears fragrant cream-colored flowers in spring, followed by tiny black berries. Useful as a hedge or screen, it grows in most soils in sun or light shade.　AREAS: ☐☐ D E ☐☐ J

P. laurocerasus and varieties
(cherry laurel, English laurel)
Handsome, dark, leathery 3- to 6-inch leaves are the hallmark of the cherry laurel. It grows 10 to 20 feet tall, is often used as a clipped hedge, but is even better unsheared as a screen.　AREAS: ☐☐ D ☐☐ I J

P. lusitanica (Portugal laurel)
In gardens the Portugal laurel usually grows as a shrub 6 to 20 feet tall. It bears clusters of white flowers in spring and purplish berries in summer.　AREAS: ☐☐☐☐☐☐ I ☐

PYRACANTHA
P. coccinea and varieties (fire thorn)
Fire thorn, a mounding thorny shrub that grows 8 to 12 feet tall, is notable for its profusion of red or orange berries, which make a colorful display in fall and winter. Clusters of tiny white flowers open in spring. Fire thorns can be used individually or in hedges. Two excellent varieties are *P. coccinea* 'Kasan,' which has red-orange berries, and *P. coccinea* 'Lalandei,' Laland fire thorn, which has handsome, bright orange fruit. Plants thrive in full sun in almost any well-drained soil.　AREAS: ☐ C D E ☐ G ☐ I J

RHODODENDRON (RHODODENDRON, AZALEA)
Like their deciduous relatives *(page 118)*, evergreen rhododendrons and azaleas provide impressive floral displays in spring; they grow best in moist, acid, organically rich soil in full sun or light shade.

R. carolinianum (Carolina rhododendron)
This early-blooming species grows slowly to 6 feet and bears rosy purple to white flowers; its leaves are up to 3 inches long with brown undersides.　AREAS: ☐ C D ☐☐☐ I ☐

R. hybrids (including Catawba, Dexter, Fortune and Shammarello hybrids)
These popular hybrids have slender leathery leaves, 4 to 8 inches long, and in spring bear magnificent clusters of white, pink, red, purple, yellow or multicolored blossoms 6 to 8 inches or more across. Plants grow 5 to 10 feet tall with an equal spread. They do best in cool climates and higher altitudes.　AREAS: ☐ C D ☐☐☐ I ☐

R. evergreen hybrids (evergreen hybrid azalea)
Most of the handsome evergreen azaleas that provide a blaze of color in spring gardens are hybrids. Horticulturists have developed a number of strains such as Gable,

Key letters refer to growing areas shown on map, page 154.

LALAND FIRE THORN
Pyracantha coccinea 'Lalandei'

EVERESTIANUM CATAWBA RHODODENDRON
Rhododendron catawbiense 'Everestianum'

ELIZABETH AZALEA
Rhododendron 'Elizabeth' *(evergreen hybrid azalea)*

Glenn Dale and Kurume hybrids that are mostly low, spreading plants 2 to 6 feet tall, characterized by unbelievable numbers of tiny flowers, which hide the small, dark green leaves. Colors range from pure white through shades of pink to red and purple. The Japanese variety *R. obtusum kaempferi* (torch azalea) often grows 5 to 6 feet tall, with an equal spread, and bears salmon pink to deep red flowers. AREAS: | | |C|D|E| | |I|J|

R. indicum and varieties (Indian azalea)
Indian azaleas grow 5 to 7 feet tall and bear 3-inch flower clusters that range from salmon pink to scarlet or white depending on the variety. AREAS: | | | |D|E| | |I|J|

R. maximum (rosebay rhododendron)
Rosebay rhododendron is the tallest of the genus (12 to 36 feet). Notable chiefly for its long narrow leaves and the fact that it blossoms about two weeks later than other rhododendrons, it is frequently used as a high evergreen background or screen; its pink flowers are small and are partly hidden by new foliage. AREAS: | |B|C|D| | | |I| |

RICE-PAPER PLANT See *Tetrapanax*
ROCK SPRAY See *Cotoneaster*
ROSE OF CHINA See *Hibiscus*
SEA GRAPE See *Coccoloba*
SHORE GRAPE See *Coccoloba*
SILVERBERRY See *Elaeagnus*

SKIMMIA
S. japonica (Japanese skimmia)
Only female plants bear the large bright red berries that distinguish this 3- to 4-foot shade-loving shrub. Both sexes produce fragrant white flowers in spring. Skimmia is often used as rough-textured ground cover in front of larger plants. AREAS: | | |D| | | |I| | |

SPANISH BROOM See *Spartium*

SPARTIUM
S. junceum (Spanish broom)
An upright shrub with sparse, bluish green foliage, Spanish broom grows 6 to 10 feet tall if unpruned and produces masses of yellow blooms in midsummer. It does best in full sun. AREAS: | | |D| | | |I|J|

TEA TREE See *Leptospermum*

TETRAPANAX, also called **FATSIA**
T. papyriferus, also called *Fatsia papyrifera*
(rice-paper plant)
A fast-growing shrub that reaches 10 to 15 feet, the rice-paper plant has immense (1- to 2-foot), deeply lobed gray-green leaves that are whitish and felty on the undersides. The bold foliage makes it a natural choice for tropical effects. Clusters of small, yellowish white flowers up to 3 feet long appear in late fall. It will grow in nearly any soil and prefers light shade. AREAS: | | | |E| | | | |J|

THEVETIA
T. peruviana, also called *T. nereifolia* (yellow oleander)
A graceful, spreading shrub 6 to 10 feet tall, yellow oleander has abundant, willowlike, dark green foliage and bears 2- to 3-inch, bell-like, fragrant yellow flowers intermittently throughout the year. Its black 1-inch fruits are poisonous. It is widely used as a hedge or ornamental plant, and tolerates heat and drought. The plant is recommended only for warmer regions. AREAS: | | | |E| | | | |J|

INDIAN AZALEA
Rhododendron indicum

TIBOUCHINA, also called **PLEROMA**
T. urvilleana, also called *T. semidecandra* and *Pleroma grandiflora* (princess flower)
This handsome, vigorous, upright shrub usually grows 5 to 15 feet tall, with velvety, heavily veined oval leaves that are reddish when young. It bears deep purple, 3-inch flowers in clusters all summer and fall. The species is recommended for warmer regions.   AREAS: | | | |E| | | |J|

VACCINIUM
V. ovatum (box blueberry, evergreen huckleberry)
Box blueberry, whose glossy leaves are coppery bronze when young, bears small white or pink flowers in spring, followed by attractive black berries that make tasty pies and jelly. Plants grow in sun or shade to a height of 2 to 8 feet and are excellent choices for hedges or background plantings. They are pest and disease free and grow well in poor acid soil.   AREAS: | | | | | | |I|

VIBURNUM
Evergreen viburnums offer, in addition to flowers and fruit, a year-round display of handsome foliage. They are useful in backgrounds, as hedges and screens, and in plantings around a house. *(See also Deciduous shrubs, page 119.)*

V. odoratissimum (sweet viburnum)
As its name implies, sweet viburnum is particularly noted for the fragrance of its white blossoms in spring, followed by clusters of berries, first red, and later black. Its large glossy leaves rival those of rhododendrons, for which it makes a good warm-climate substitute. Plants grow 8 to 10 feet tall or more.   AREAS: | | |E| | | |J|

V. rhytidophyllum (leatherleaf viburnum)
Massive crinkled leaves adorn this species, which grows to a height of 6 to 12 feet or more. Clusters of white flowers appear in spring, followed by berries that turn red, then black as they mature. Plants should be situated out of wind.   AREAS: | | |D| | |I|J|

V. tinus (laurestinus)
Luxuriant foliage makes this shrub a favorite screen or hedge plant, especially if it is not pruned. Plants grow 6 to 12 feet tall and bear white flower clusters in late winter or early spring, followed by blue berries, which cling until late in the year. Laurestinus is recommended for the northern part of Area E.   AREAS: | | |D|E| | |I|J|

WILD LILAC See *Ceanothus*
WINTER CREEPER See *Euonymus*

XYLOSMA, also called **MYROXYLON**
X. senticosa, also called *Myroxylon congestum* (xylosma)
The glistening green foliage of this fine shrub is bronze tinted when young and remains handsome regardless of heat or drought. Plants grow 8 to 10 feet tall and can be used in hedges or screens.   AREAS: | | | | | | | |J|

YAUPON See *Ilex*
YELLOW OLEANDER See *Thevetia*
YESTERDAY, TODAY AND TOMORROW
  See *Brunfelsia*

Ground covers

Ground covers, plants with a low, spreading growth habit, are among the most practical and beautiful of landscaping materials, yet their potentials are fre-

XYLOSMA
Xylosma senticosa

Key letters refer to growing areas shown on map, page 154.

quently overlooked by homeowners. Bordering a path, cloaking a bank, decorating a rock garden or planted in luxuriant beds for their own sake, they can provide delightful contrasts in texture and color to adjoining areas of grass or paving; used as a low background, they can tie together and set off plantings of shrubs, flowers or trees. Many ground covers are invaluable in locations where grass will not grow—in extremely dry soil, for example, or in the dense shade beneath a tree—and many are suited to steep banks where erosion is a problem and where grass is hard to mow. Some, like bugleweed, grow rapidly; plants set 12 inches apart will grow together into a dense mass within a year. Others, like bearberry, are slow growing, taking several years to form an uninterrupted texture. Most ground covers, once they are established, require little or no care.

AEGOPODIUM

A. podagraria variegatum (silveredge bishop's weed, silveredge goutweed)
This sturdy perennial with coarse, sawtooth-edged green and white leaves grows 8 to 10 inches high but dies to the ground in fall. Able to thrive in any soil, in shade and all but the most intense sunlight, it spreads rapidly by underground roots. AREAS: B C D F G H I

AJUGA

A. reptans and varieties (bugleweed, carpet bugle)
Low lying (4 to 6 inches high) and perennial, bugleweed forms a dense carpet of small oval leaves in sunny or shady areas. Some varieties' leaves are bronze, purplish red or splashed with white or pink. Clusters of small blue, purplish, reddish or white flowers appear on slender stems in spring and early summer. AREAS: B C D F G H I J

ARCTOSTAPHYLOS

A. uva-ursi (bearberry, kinnikinnick)
A trailing evergreen shrub with small, shiny green leaves that turn bronze in winter, bearberry grows 6 to 12 inches high and is useful as a covering for rocky or sandy slopes. It is slow growing and drought resistant, thriving in sun or moderate shade in poor or acid soils that are well drained. Tiny, bell-shaped whitish pink flowers appear in spring, followed by bright red berries. AREAS: A B C F H I J

BEARBERRY See *Arctostaphylos*
BISHOP'S WEED See *Aegopodium*
BUGLEWEED See *Ajuga*
CARPET BUGLE See *Ajuga*
CREEPING MYRTLE See *Vinca*

DICHONDRA

D. micrantha, also called *D. repens* (dichondra)
Dichondra, a popular substitute for grass in West Coast lawns, grows up to 6 inches high and can be mowed back to 1 or 2 inches. The rich green color and smooth texture of its tiny kidney-shaped perennial leaves offer a striking contrast to concrete and other paving materials. Like grass, dichondra reseeds itself and spreads by underground runners. It does best in frost-free areas. AREAS: J

EUONYMUS

(See also Deciduous shrubs, page 115, Broad-leaved evergreen shrubs, page 138, and Vines, page 150.)
E. fortunei coloratus (purple winter creeper)
A trailing evergreen vine often used as a ground cover, purple winter creeper provides a strong 6-inch-high carpet of

BUGLEWEED, CARPET BUGLE
Ajuga reptans

ENGLISH IVY
Hedera helix

WILTON CARPET JUNIPER
Juniperus horizontalis wiltonii

146

small, oval, glossy green leaves that turn a distinctive reddish purple in fall and winter. It thrives in sun or shade, roots along its stems, and is often used on steep slopes to prevent soil erosion. AREAS: | | B | C | D | | F | G | H | I | J |

FRAGARIA (STRAWBERRY)
F. chiloensis (sand strawberry)
Abundant white flowers and lush, dark, evergreen leaves characterize this plant in spring. Small edible berries follow the flowers. Plants grow 6 to 12 inches tall and spread rapidly by runners; they need full or partial sun and grow in many soils, including sand. AREAS: | | | | | | | | | I | J |

GOUTWEED See *Aegopodium*

HEDERA (IVY)
(See also Vines, page 150.)
H. helix (English ivy)
English ivy, widely used as a climbing vine, also makes an excellent evergreen ground cover for sunny or shady areas. It grows best in deeply prepared, moist soil with an abundance of organic matter. AREAS: | | | C | D | E | | G | | I | J |

HOLLY GRAPE See *Mahonia*
IVY See *Hedera*

JUNIPERUS (JUNIPER)
(See also Narrow-leaved evergreen shrubs, page 132.)
J. horizontalis wiltonii (Wilton carpet juniper)
The flattest of the creeping junipers, the *wiltonii* variety rarely exceeds 4 inches in height, spreading as much as 8 to 10 feet to form a wavy mass of bright, silver-blue needlelike foliage. Striking in rock gardens or borders, it needs little care and withstands hot sun and winter frost, but needs well-drained soil. AREAS: | A | B | C | D | | F | G | H | I | J |

KINNIKINNICK See *Arctostaphylos*
LIVE-FOREVER See *Sedum*

MAHONIA
(See also Broad-leaved evergreen shrubs, page 141.)
M. repens (creeping mahonia, dwarf holly grape)
A highly ornamental evergreen that has hollylike, bluish green leaves, creeping mahonia grows less than 12 inches high, bearing spikes of small yellow flowers in spring and tiny, black, grapelike fruit in summer. It spreads by underground roots, does well in sun or shade and grows vigorously in moist rich soil. AREAS: | | | C | D | | | | I | J |

MYRTLE, CREEPING See *Vinca*
MYRTLE, TRAILING See *Vinca*

PACHISTIMA, also called PAXISTIMA
(See also Broad-leaved evergreen shrubs, page 142.)
P. canbyi (Canby pachistima)
A shrubby evergreen that grows about a foot high, this species has handsome, dense, small-leaved foliage, bronzed in fall, that goes well with larger broad-leaved evergreens such as rhododendrons. It does best in a moist acid soil and grows well in shade. AREAS: | | | C | D | | | | I |

PACHYSANDRA
P. terminalis (Japanese pachysandra, Japanese spurge)
Japanese pachysandra has rich evergreen leaves that form a dense tapestry in borders and edgings, growing to 10 inches high. It is valued for its ability to thrive in deep shade, on the north side of houses and under trees with heavy foliage and shallow roots. AREAS: | | B | C | D | | F | G | H | I | J |

Key letters refer to growing areas shown on map, page 154.

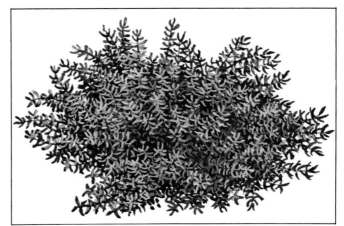

CANBY PACHISTIMA
Pachistima canbyi

JAPANESE PACHYSANDRA, JAPANESE SPURGE
Pachysandra terminalis

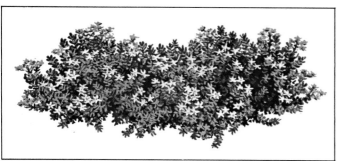
WHITE STONECROP
Sedum album

COMMON PERIWINKLE, CREEPING MYRTLE
Vinca minor

BARBARA KARST BOUGAINVILLEA
Bougainvillea 'Barbara Karst'

PERIWINKLE See *Vinca*

SEDUM (STONECROP, LIVE-FOREVER)

Most sedums are evergreen perennials only a few inches high with small, thick, juice-filled leaves that are especially decorative in rock gardens. Some species are creeping or trailing, others upright or tufted; most produce quantities of star-shaped, white, yellow, pink or red flowers. Plants require little care but cannot be walked on because their leaves crush easily. Sedum grows well in sun and almost any soil. AREAS: A B C D E F G H I J

SPURGE See *Pachysandra*
STONECROP See *Sedum*
STRAWBERRY See *Fragaria*
TRAILING MYRTLE See *Vinca*

VINCA (PERIWINKLE)

V. minor (common periwinkle, trailing myrtle, creeping myrtle)
The small, tapered, glossy green leaves of this evergreen ground cover grow on trailing stems to a height of 6 inches. In early spring, many small, star-shaped, lilac-blue, purple or white flowers appear. Periwinkle roots where it touches the ground, and does best in light shade and moist rich soil. AREAS: B C D F G H I J

WINTER CREEPER See *Euonymus*

Vines

Vines can be used purely as ornaments, climbing up a tree trunk or twining around a doorway pillar; in addition to their decorative leaf patterns, many are noted for their flowers. They can also serve many practical landscape functions—forming a shade-giving roof on the latticework over a patio, cloaking a rainspout or a barren wall, converting an open fence into a privacy screen, even trailing rampant to become a thick, matted ground cover.

In choosing a vine for a particular purpose, it is important first to consider how the vine climbs. Some vines, like five-leaf akebia, simply twine themselves around a support such as a trellis or a rail fence. Others send out leafless tendrils that coil around supports such as wire fences or wires attached to a wall. Still others literally stick to the surfaces they climb on by means of adhesive "holdfasts" or discs.

ACTINIDIA

A. arguta (bower actinidia, tara vine)
This twining deciduous vine grows quickly to 30 feet, providing dense screening over fences and trellises. Its 5-inch, glossy, dark green, red-stemmed leaves appear in early spring. Small fragrant white flowers are followed on female plants in midsummer by yellow-green 1-inch fruit that may be used in preserves. The vines thrive in moist soil, in full sun or partial shade. AREAS: B C D E F G H I J

AKEBIA

A. quinata (five-leaf akebia)
This delicate twining vine has semievergreen fingerlike leaves and fragrant, purple spring flowers. Fast growing to a length of 25 to 35 feet, it makes an attractive screen over fences, trellises or wires and can be used to cover rainspouts. It thrives in sun or light shade and is highly pest and disease resistant. Unsupported, it becomes a thick ground cover. AREAS: C D E G H I J

AMPELOPSIS See *Parthenocissus*
ANISOSTICHUS See *Bignonia*

BIGNONIA
B. capreolata, also called *Anisostichus capreolatus,*
Doxantha capreolata (crossvine, trumpet flower)
The evergreen crossvine is fast growing to 60 feet in length,
clings by disc-ended tendrils and bears an abundance of
1½- to 2-inch trumpet-shaped orange-red flowers in late
spring and early summer. Its bright green foliage turns reddish green in fall and winter, making an attractive year-
round screen. It thrives in moist well-drained soil in full
sun or partial shade.   AREAS: | | |D|E| |G| |J|

BITTERSWEET See *Celastrus*
BOSTON IVY See *Parthenocissus*

BOUGAINVILLEA
B. hybrids (bougainvillea)
These handsome ornamental evergreen vines sprawl over
walls or fences, clinging with hooked spines and rapidly
reaching 15 to 25 feet or more in length. Pegged down,
they make fine ground covers. Bright red, yellowish orange, purple, pink or white flowerlike bracts surround tiny
inconspicuous flowers, which bloom all year. *B.* hybrids,
recommended only for warmer regions, do best in full sun
and well-drained soil.   AREAS: | | | |E| | | |J|

CAMPSIS (TRUMPET VINE)
C. tagliabuana 'Madame Galen'
(Madame Galen trumpet vine)
Spectacular clusters of trumpet-shaped, orange to red flowers, about 3 inches across, bloom in midsummer on this fast-
growing deciduous vine, which attracts hummingbirds. It
reaches 25 to 30 feet, has coarse, dark green leaves, and
clings by rootlike holdfasts that withstand high winds. It
thrives in full sun and moist well-drained soil and is highly
pest resistant.   AREAS: |B|C|D|E| |G|H|I|J|

CAROLINA JASMINE See *Gelsemium*

CELASTRUS (BITTERSWEET)
C. scandens (American bittersweet)
Twining American bittersweet, a deciduous vine, rambles
along walls and fences or provides a lush ground cover. It
grows rapidly to 20 feet and must be confined to specific
areas lest it smother nearby plants and young trees. In
fall, female plants produce orange-yellow fruit capsules
that split open, revealing bright red berries. Since male
plants are needed to fertilize blossoms, plant a male and fe-
male in the same hole.   AREAS: |A|B|C|D| |F|G|H|I|J|

CLEMATIS
These exquisite, usually fast-growing flowering vines curl
tendril-like leaflets around any small object in their path.
They do well on wires, stout strings or light wooden trellises; the more rampant growers may simply be allowed to
scramble over a stump or wall. Clematis do best in moist,
light, slightly alkaline loam and full sun or partial shade.
No other plants should be cultivated near them since their
roots are shallow. The clematises listed are deciduous.

C. hybrids (hybrid clematis)
Hybrid clematis bloom in summer in a range of colors and
reach heights of 6 to 15 feet. Typical varieties are 'Ramona' (blue to purple), 'Comtesse de Bouchard' (pink),
'Crimson Star' (red), 'Duchess of Edinburgh' (white) and
C. jackmanii (purple).   AREAS: |B|C|D| |F|G|H|I|J|

Key letters refer to growing areas shown on map, page 154.

MADAME GALEN TRUMPET VINE
Campsis tagliabuana 'Madame Galen'

RAMONA CLEMATIS
Clematis 'Ramona'

PINK ANEMONE CLEMATIS
Clematis montana rubens

CAROLINA JASMINE
Gelsemium sempervirens

C. montana rubens (pink anemone clematis)
The pink anemone clematis grows at a moderate rate to a height of 15 to 25 feet and bears fragrant, 2- to 2½-inch rosy pink flowers in late spring.   AREAS: ☐ C D ☐ G H I J

CONFEDERATE JASMINE See *Trachelospermum*
CREEPER See *Parthenocissus*
CROSSVINE See *Bignonia*
DOXANTHA See *Bignonia*

EUONYMUS
(See also Deciduous shrubs, page 115, Broad-leaved ever-green shrubs, page 138, and Ground covers, page 146.)
E. fortunei radicans (common winter creeper)
A slow-growing evergreen that may reach 15 to 25 feet after many years, this vine trails and climbs, attaching it-self with aerial holdfasts. It thrives in well-drained moist soils, in sun or shade. Pink fruit capsules open in fall to re-veal orange berries.   AREAS: ☐ B C D ☐ F G H I J

FICUS (FIG)
(See also Broad-leaved evergreen trees, page 128.)
F. pumila (creeping fig)
The creeping fig rapidly forms a thick dense blanket of oval evergreen leaves. The stems of the vine, which criss-cross, produce small erect branches that bear inedible figs. The vine does best in moist soil, in sun or shade and may grow 20 to 60 feet in height.   AREAS: ☐ ☐ E ☐ ☐ J

FLEECE VINE See *Polygonum*

GELSEMIUM
G. sempervirens (Carolina jasmine)
A sprawling evergreen vine with 1- to 3-inch green leaves, the Carolina jasmine grows 20 to 35 feet tall and bears clus-ters of fragrant, tubelike, 1½-inch yellow flowers in early spring. It does well in moist well-drained soil in full sun or partial shade.   AREAS: ☐ ☐ D E ☐ ☐ J

HEDERA (IVY)
Ivies are fast-growing evergreen vines that serve equally well as ground covers *(page 147)*. Clinging by small aerial rootlets, they can climb to heights of 50 feet or more; older vines bear clusters of tiny greenish white flowers in fall, followed by black berries in spring. Ivies thrive in rich moist soil and sun, but do best in partial shade.

H. canariensis (Algerian ivy)
Algerian ivy has unusually large, handsome leaves, up to 7 inches in diameter, and makes a highly decorative vine on walls and fences.   AREAS: ☐ ☐ D E ☐ ☐ J

H. helix (English ivy)
One of the most popular of all evergreen vines, English ivy will grow 50 to 90 feet tall if unchecked. Its dull green leaves, 2 to 4 inches across, normally have three to five lobes.   AREAS: ☐ C D E ☐ G ☐ I J

HONEYSUCKLE See *Lonicera*

HYDRANGEA
(See also Deciduous shrubs, page 116.)
H. anomala petiolaris, also called *H. petiolaris*,
H. scandens (climbing hydrangea)
Spectacular white flowers in large, flat clusters clothe these deciduous vines in midsummer. They grow slowly when young but more rapidly when established, and may reach 75 feet, climbing over boulders, walls and tree trunks. Their aerial rootlets should be kept away from wooden surfaces.

Climbing hydrangeas thrive in moist soil in full sun or partial shade.   AREAS: ☐ C D E ☐ G H I J

IVY See *Hedera*
IVY, BOSTON See *Parthenocissus*
JASMINE See *Jasminum*
JASMINE, CAROLINA See *Gelsemium*
JASMINE, CONFEDERATE See *Trachelospermum*
JASMINE, STAR See *Trachelospermum*

JASMINUM (JASMINE)
(See also Broad-leaved evergreen shrubs, page 140.)
J. mesnyi, also called *J. primulinum* (primrose jasmine)
The evergreen primrose jasmine grows as a mound of slender, arching branches 10 to 15 feet tall unless tied to a trellis or wall. It has shiny, dark green leaves and in spring bears 1½- to 2-inch yellow flowers that are slightly fragrant. The vines grow in moist well-drained soil, in full sun or partial shade.   AREAS: ☐☐ D E ☐ G ☐☐ J

LACE VINE See *Polygonum*

LONICERA (HONEYSUCKLE)
(See also Deciduous shrubs, page 117, and Broad-leaved evergreen shrubs, page 141.)
L. sempervirens and varieties (trumpet honeysuckle)
Trumpet-shaped orange, scarlet or yellow flower clusters bloom in summer and fall on 15- to 20-foot twining vines that are useful on walls or as a ground cover. Semievergreen in northern areas, they thrive in moist well-drained soil in sun or partial shade.   AREAS: ☐ B C D E F G H I J

PARTHENOCISSUS, also called AMPELOPSIS
These two fast-growing, deciduous creepers do well in moist, well-drained soil in full sun or partial shade. Blue-black berries appear in fall.

P. quinquefolia (Virginia creeper, woodbine)
Climbing by tendrils equipped with rootlike holdfasts, these graceful vines, which can grow to 50 feet tall, send out slender, pendant side branches of uneven lengths that wave in the slightest breeze. The five-fingered leaves turn brilliant scarlet in early fall.   AREAS: ☐ B C D E F G H I J

P. tricuspidata (Boston ivy, Japanese creeper)
The thick, glossy leaves of Boston ivy, shaped somewhat like maple leaves and tinged a faint red, turn orange and scarlet in fall. Vines may grow 60 feet tall, clinging to solid surfaces with highly adhesive, disk-tipped tendrils that can damage wooden walls.   AREAS: ☐ B C D E ☐ G H I J

POLYGONUM
P. aubertii (silver fleece vine, silver lace vine)
This deciduous vine grows 15 to 30 feet tall and is blanketed with clouds of small, fluffy white flowers from early spring to late summer. It is highly pest and drought resistant; if killed to the ground by severe frost, it will grow back from the roots.   AREAS: ☐ B C D E F G H I J

RHYNCHOSPERMUM See *Trachelospermum*
STAR JASMINE See *Trachelospermum*
TARA VINE See *Actinidia*

TRACHELOSPERMUM,
also called RHYNCHOSPERMUM
T. jasminoides (star jasmine, Confederate jasmine)
The long, shiny dark green leaves of this evergreen twining vine, which grows 10 to 20 feet tall, form thick screens,

Key letters refer to growing areas shown on map, page 154.

CLIMBING HYDRANGEA
Hydrangea anomala petiolaris

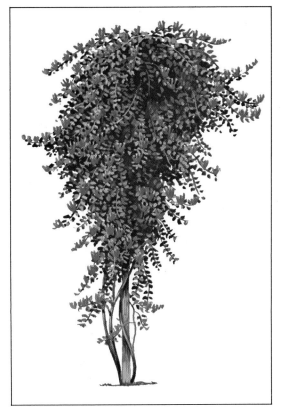
TRUMPET HONEYSUCKLE
Lonicera sempervirens

on which small, fragrant white flowers bloom in summer. The vines require moist soil and full or partial shade and make durable ground covers. AREAS: ☐☐☐E☐☐☐J

TRUMPET FLOWER See *Bignonia*
TRUMPET VINE See *Campsis*
WINTER CREEPER See *Euonymus*

WISTERIA

Most wisterias are fast-growing, twining, deciduous vines that climb as high as 40 feet over tall arbors or sturdy trellises. Long clusters of delicately fragrant flowers appear in spring, just before the leaves unfold. Occasional flowers may appear later in the season. Wisterias do best in full sun in rich well-drained soil.

W. floribunda and varieties (Japanese wisteria)
This species bears white, pink or purplish flowers in clusters up to 3 feet long. AREAS: ☐☐CDE☐G☐IJ

W. sinensis, also called *W. chinensis* (Chinese wisteria)
The pea-shaped violet-blue flowers of these vines open all at once, making a grand display in spring. *W. sinensis alba* has fragrant white flowers. AREAS: ☐☐CDE☐G☐IJ

WOODBINE See *Parthenocissus*

Palms

Palm trees are a special, and often dramatic, landscaping feature of a fringe of the United States that begins north of San Francisco and continues through California, parts of the Southwest and Texas, and along the Gulf Coast to include Florida. While most palms have straight or slightly curving single trunks, some species grow in clumps of several trunks. The leaves of some are fan shaped; in others they are long, arching, featherlike fronds. Most palms do best in rich soil with plenty of water and fertilizer. Although they do not tolerate persistent frost, quite a number are surprisingly hardy; temperature tolerances are indicated for each species.

ARECA See *Chrysalidocarpus*

ARECASTRUM

A. romanzoffianum, also called *Cocos plumosa*
(queen palm)
A commanding ornamental tree with a straight, silvery trunk and a crown of elegant "feather-duster" fronds 10 to 15 feet long, the queen palm may grow to 40 feet in 30 years. Four- to 5-foot clusters of yellow flowers in summer are followed by showy, inedible 1-inch fruit. Queen palms are recommended only for warm areas out of high winds; they will tolerate temperatures to the low 20s, although the fronds will become browned. AREAS: ☐☐☐E☐☐☐J

BAMBOO PALM See *Chrysalidocarpus*
BUTTERFLY PALM See *Chrysalidocarpus*
CANE PALM See *Chrysalidocarpus*

CHAMAEROPS

C. humilis (European fan palm, Mediterranean fan palm)
This slow-growing palm usually reaches 6 to 12 feet in height in a clump of curving trunks, each supporting a rounded head of stiff fan-shaped leaves. It makes a stunning sculptural element in a garden and can be grown in patio containers. One of the hardiest palms, surviving tempera-

CHINESE WISTERIA
Wisteria sinensis

QUEEN PALM
Arecastrum romanzoffianum

tures to 6° F., it grows best in moist rich soil, but tolerates drought. AREAS:☐☐☐E☐☐☐I☐J

CHAMAEROPS EXCELSA See *Trachycarpus*

CHRYSALIDOCARPUS
C. lutescens, also called *Areca lutescens* (butterfly palm, yellow palm, bamboo palm, Areca palm, cane palm)
This 20- to 40-foot palm, grown only in southern Florida, Hawaii and warm coastal areas of California, has bamboolike canes topped by pliant, light green 6- to 8-foot fronds. Fragrant white flowers on spikes are followed by small, blackish inedible fruit. Butterfly palms make exotic specimens for pots, patio or lawn, screens or backgrounds. They need rich soil and plenty of water; they tolerate shade, but very little frost. AREAS:☐☐☐E☐☐☐☐J

COCOS PLUMOSA See *Arecastrum*
DATE PALM See *Phoenix*
EUROPEAN FAN PALM See *Chamaerops*
LADY PALM See *Rhapis*
MEDITERRANEAN FAN PALM See *Chamaerops*

PHOENIX (DATE PALM)
P. reclinata, also called *P. natalensis, P. senegalensis, P. spinosa, P. spinifera* (Senegal date palm)
This tall, slender, multitrunked species grows rapidly to 25 to 35 feet. Its feathery, glistening green fronds arch gracefully over the trunks, which are rough with old leaf bases. Inconspicuous cream-colored flowers are followed on female trees by sticky orange dates, edible but not very tasty. The Senegal palm is striking alone and combines well with other tropical plants. It grows in full sun or partial shade in well-drained soils, but tolerates very little frost (27° to 28° F.). AREAS:☐☐☐E☐☐☐☐J

P. roebelenii, also called *P. loueiri*
(dwarf date palm, pigmy date palm)
Often used in gardens, and indoors as a fernlike plant when young, this species grows only 6 to 8 feet tall. Its 3- to 4-foot arching fronds resemble luxuriant plumes. Female plants grow inconspicuous flowers and inch-long, black, edible dates. The dwarf date palm can stand desert heat but only occasional light frost. AREAS:☐☐☐E☐☐☐J

QUEEN PALM See *Arecastrum*

RHAPIS
R. excelsa, also called *R. flabelliformis* (lady palm)
The bamboolike lady palm grows about 5 feet tall, with dense, broad fan-shaped leaves spreading above stiff, reedy stems of varying heights. It is often used in containers, against a fence or wall, or with other plantings. It requires some shade and fertile, well-drained soil and withstands temperatures to 20° F. AREAS:☐☐☐E☐☐☐J

TRACHYCARPUS
T. fortunei, also called *T. excelsus, Chamaerops excelsa* (windmill palm)
This species bears yard-broad leaves whose stiff leaflets fan out in a windmill pattern above a slender upright trunk covered with brown or black fibers. Slow growing to 15 to 35 feet, it is often used as a tub plant, lawn or patio ornament. One of the hardiest palms, it survives temperatures as low as 10° F. AREAS:☐☐☐E☐☐☐J

WINDMILL PALM See *Trachycarpus*
YELLOW PALM See *Chrysalidocarpus*

Key letters refer to growing areas shown on map, page 154.

BUTTERFLY PALM
Chrysalidocarpus lutescens

DWARF DATE PALM, PIGMY DATE PALM
Phoenix roebelenii

LADY PALM
Rhapis excelsa

Appendix

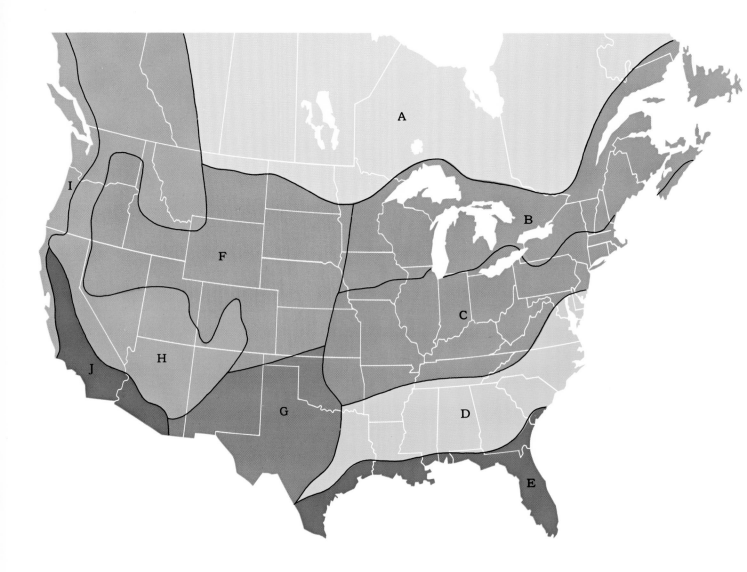

Where recommended plants will thrive

This map, devised by the author as a broad general guide to landscape planting, divides the U.S. and southern Canada into 10 areas, identified by letters, on the basis of prevailing temperatures, rainfall, altitude and types of soil. It is meant to be used with the encyclopedia of plant materials (Chapter 5). Each encyclopedia entry indicates the best areas for the listed plant, but with care many will also thrive in other areas.

Conditions vary from place to place within each region, however, and it is always wise to consult your nurseryman about the advisability of using particular plants in your locality. Area C, for example, is probably the most homogeneous in

terms of climate, and is hospitable to the widest range of plants. But even within Area C the central part of the Allegheny Mountain region is colder and rainier than Long Island, and within Long Island, winds from the Atlantic Ocean make it more difficult to grow certain plants in the eastern portion than in the west. Area I is one of the easiest regions to garden in; it enjoys moderate year-round temperatures, generally good soil, ample moisture and an optimum amount of sunshine. Area A, on the other hand, is the hardest on plants; because of its subzero winter temperatures and winds, only hardy coniferous evergreens and a limited number of deciduous trees and shrubs can do well there.

Picture Credits

The sources for the illustrations that appear in this book are listed below. Credits for the pictures from left to right are separated by semicolons, from top to bottom by dashes. Photographers' names appear in parentheses when they follow the names of landscape architects and designers.

Cover—Garden design by Guy Greene, Tucson, Ariz. (Dean Brown). 4—Keith Martin courtesy James Underwood Crockett. 6—Dean Brown. 10, 13—Drawings by Vincent Lewis. 17—Courtesy the Metropolitan Museum of Art (Robert Crandall Assoc.). 18, 19—Colonial Williamsburg Photograph—Sheldon Cotler (2). 20—Enrico Ferorelli. 21—Rare Book Division, New York Public Library, from *The Gardeners Labyrinth,* Hill, 1608—Enrico Ferorelli. 22, 23—Courtesy Hispanic Society of America, from *Les Délices de l'Espagne et du Portugal,* Pieter van der Aa, 1715 (Robert Crandall Assoc.)—Stewart E. King Associates, Landscape Architects, San Antonio (Enrico Ferorelli—2). 24—Royston, Hanamoto, Beck & Abey, Landscape Architects, Campbell & Wong Architects, San Francisco (Dean Brown). 29—Drawing by Vincent Lewis. 31—Drawing adapted by Vincent Lewis from *Influence of a Field Windbreak on Summer Wind Movement and Air Temperature,* Kansas State University Agricultural Experiment Station, Technical Bulletin 100, June 1959. 34—Adapted by Vincent Lewis from drawing on page 144 of the *Land Development Manual,* National Association of Home Builders, 1969. 39—Charles Gillette, Landscape Architect, Richmond, Va. (Leonard Wolfe). 40, 41—Arthur Berger, Landscape Architect, Dallas (Dean Brown). 42—Isabel De C. Porter, Landscape Architect, Beverly Farms, Mass. (Richard Meek)—Reich-Earle-Cuellar, Landscape Architects, Baton Rouge (Dean Brown—2). 43—Wertheim & van der Ploeg, Landscape Architects, San Francisco (Dean Brown)—Dean Brown—Lewis Clarke Associates, Landscape Architects, Raleigh, N.C. (Enrico Ferorelli). 44, 45—Stewart E. King & Associates, Landscape Architects, Ford, Powell & Carson, Architects, San Antonio (Enrico Ferorelli). 46—Clarence Roy, Landscape Architect, Ann Arbor (Dean Brown). 47, 48, 49—Landscape design by Allen C. Haskell, New Bedford, Mass. (Dean Brown). 50, 51—Allan Grant; Jack C. Stafford, Landscape Architect, Palo Alto (Dean Brown)—Landscape design by Leon Pearson, Hooksett, N.H. (Richard Meek). 52, 53—K. C. Ka-

wamoto, Landscape Architect, Thomas D. Church, Landscape Architect, San Francisco (Fred Lyon from Rapho Guillumette). 54, 55—Stewart E. King & Associates, Landscape Architects, Ford, Powell & Carson, Architects, San Antonio (Dean Brown); Reich-Earle-Cuellar, Landscape Architects, Baton Rouge (Dean Brown). 56—William G. Teufel, Landscape Architect, Seattle (Dean Brown); Stewart E. King & Glenn Cook, Landscape Architects, San Antonio (Dean Brown). 57—Eriksson, Peters & Thoms, Landscape Architects, Pasadena (Dean Brown); Chandler D. Fairbank, Landscape Architect, Portland, Ore. (Dean Brown). 58—Chandler D. Fairbank, Landscape Architect, Portland, Ore. (Dean Brown); Landscape design by Allen C. Haskell, New Bedford, Mass. (Dean Brown). 59—Hahn, Hoffman, Schmidt, Landscape Architects, Pasadena (Dean Brown); Landscape design by Eric Paepcke, Washington, D.C. (Farrell Grehan). 60, 61, 62—Hahn, Hoffman, Schmidt, Landscape Architects, Pasadena (Dean Brown). 65, 67—Drawings by Vincent Lewis. 71—Stewart E. King & Associates, Landscape Architects, Ford, Powell & Carson, Architects, San Antonio (Enrico Ferorelli). 72—Enrico Ferorelli—Farrell Grehan—Sebastian Milito. 73—Dean Brown except left center and left bottom, Farrell Grehan. 74, 75—Dean Brown; Landscape design by Lin Emery, New Orleans (Enrico Ferorelli). 76—Charles W. Cares, Landscape Architect, Ann Arbor (Dean Brown); Landscape design by Eric Paepcke, Washington, D.C. (Farrell Grehan). 77—Garrett Eckbo, Landscape Architect, Berkeley, Calif. (Dean Brown); Landscape design by Floyd Johnson, Charlottesville (Farrell Grehan). 78, 79—A. E. Bye Associates, Cos Cob, Conn. (Sebastian Milito). 80—Floyd Zimmerman, Landscape Architect, Watertown, Mass. (Dean Brown). 82, 84, 87—Drawings by Vincent Lewis. 89, 90, 91—Thomas D. Church, Landscape Architect, San Francisco (Dean Brown). 92—Lewis Clarke Associates, Landscape Architects, Raleigh, N.C. (Enrico Ferorelli). 94, 95—Guy Greene, Landscape Architect, Tucson (Dean Brown). 96, 97—Royston, Hanamoto, Beck & Abey, Landscape Architects, Bushnell, Jessup, Murphy & Van de Weghe, Architects, San Francisco (Dean Brown). 98—Illustration by Don Moss. 100 through 153—Illustrations by Rebecca Merrilees and Barbara Wolff. 154—Map by Adolph E. Brotman.

Acknowledgments

For their help in the preparation of this book, the editors wish to thank the following: Douglas Baylis, Landscape Architect, San Francisco; Calvin Thomas Bishop, Landscape Architect, Bishop and Walker, Landscape Architects, Houston; Houston B. Bliss, Landscape Architect, Dallas; Ray Brush, Secretary, American Association of Nurserymen, Washington, D.C.; Henry Cole, Landscape Architect, San Rafael, Calif.; Mrs. Edith Crockett, Librarian, The Horticultural Society of New York, New York City; L. A. DeMartino Jr., Landscape Architect, San Antonio; Richard W. Dickinson, Associate Executive Director, American Society of Landscape Architects, Washington, D.C.; Garrett Eckbo, Eckbo, Dean, Austin & Williams, Landscape Architects, San Francisco; Arthur W. Erfeldt, Landscape Architect, Portland, Ore.; Barbara Fealy, Landscape Architect, Portland, Ore.; E. B. Flowers, Architect, San Antonio; Chris Friedrich, Landscape Architect, New Orleans; Robert E. Goetz & Associates, Landscape Architects, Webster Groves, Mo.; Robert I. Gould, Director, Land Use and Engineering Department, National Association of Home Builders, Washington, D.C.; Richard Haag Associates, Inc., Landscape Architects, Seattle; Asa Hanamoto, Landscape Architect, Royston, Hanamoto, Beck & Abey, San Francisco; Dr. C. G. Hard, Associate Professor, Landscape Design and Environmental Planning, University of Minnesota, St. Paul, Minn.; Huntington and Roth, Landscape Architects, Portland, Ore.; Johnson, Johnson & Roy, Inc., Landscape Architects, Ann Arbor; James H. Johnson, Architect, Denver; Peter Johnson, Landscape Ar-

chitect, A. E. Bye and Associates, Cos Cob, Conn.; George A. Kalmbacher, Plant Taxonomist, Brooklyn Botanic Garden, New York; James E. Keeter, Landscape Architect, San Antonio; Mrs. Ceylon Robert Kidwell, Curator, Governor's Palace, San Antonio; Mrs. Marsha Markle, Hispanic Society of America, New York City; Vincent N. Merrill, Shurcliff, Merrill & Footit, Landscape Architects, Boston; Chris G. Moritz, Landscape Architect, Denver; Mrs. James H. Newton, Curator, Whipple House, Ipswich, Mass.; Mrs. Maynard Omerberg, Hollywood, Calif.; Donald H. Parker, Director of Landscape Architecture, Colonial Williamsburg Foundation, Williamsburg, Va.; Courtland P. Paul and Gerald Pearson, Landscape Architects, Courtland Paul, Arthur Beggs & Associates, Pasadena; Robert P. Perron, Landscape Architect, Portland, Ore.; Artemas P. Richardson, Landscape Architect, Olmsted Associates, Brookline, Mass.; D. C. Richardson, Landscape Architect, Zion & Breen Associates, New York City; Gary O. Robinette, Executive Director, American Society of Landscape Architects Foundation, Washington, D.C.; Stephen A. Scalia, New Orleans; Mrs. A. W. Smith, Ipswich, Mass.; George H. Spalding, Botanical Information Consultant, Los Angeles State and County Arboretum, Arcadia, Calif.; Edward D. Stone Jr. & Associates, Site Planners and Landscape Architects, Fort Lauderdale; Robert B. Walker, Bishop and Walker, Landscape Architects, Houston. Quotations from *Gardens Are for People,* © 1955 by Thomas Church, reprinted by permission of the publishers, Van Nostrand and Reinhold Co., New York City.

Index

Numerals in italics indicate an illustration of the subject mentioned

PRINTED IN U.S.A.